No. 331

MW01122612

Mexico's struggle with 'drugs and thugs'

Introduction 3

1. Wars and the Spread of Drugs 9

2. The Weakening of the Mexican State 23

3. Calderón's Top Priority 37

Talking It Over...62

Annotated Reading List 64

Online Resources..66

Appendix 1: Mexican Cartels 68

Appendix 2: Calderón's Major Antidrug Operations............ 86

Appendix 3: Mexico's Security Cabinet............................... 92

Cover Design: Agnieshka Burke

$8.99

Cover Photo: Reuters/Landov

The drug-smuggling tunnel under the U.S.-Mexican border.

Author

GEORGE W. GRAYSON, *who is the Class of 1938 Professor of Government at the College of William & Mary, is
a member of the Center for Immigration Studies Board
of Directors. He is also a senior associate at the Center
for Strategic & International Studies and an associate
scholar at the Foreign Policy Research Institute.*

The author wishes to express appreciation to University of Miami professor Bruce
M. Bagley and to James Creechan, a Toronto-based sociologist and criminolo-
gist at the University of Toronto and University of Guelph for providing invalu-
able comments on an earlier version of this manuscript. He is also indebted to
College of William & Mary student Gabriela Regina Arias for superb research
and editing.

The Foreign Policy Association

The Foreign Policy Association is a private, nonprofit, nonpartisan educational
organization. Its purpose is to stimulate wider interest and more effective par-
ticipation in, and greater understanding of, world affairs among American citizens. Among its activities is the continuous publication, dating from 1935, of the
HEADLINE SERIES. The author is responsible for factual accuracy and for the views
expressed. FPA itself takes no position on issues of U.S. foreign policy.

HEADLINE SERIES (ISSN 0017-8780) is published occasionally by the Foreign Policy Association, Inc., 470 Park Avenue So., New York, NY 10016. Chairman, Gonzalo de Las
Heras; President, Noel V. Lateef; Editor in Chief, Karen M. Rohan; Managing Editor,
Ann R. Monjo; Art and Production Editor, Agnieshka Burke; Associate Editor, Nicholas
Y. Barratt; Assistant Editor, Ke Wei. Subscription rates, $30.00 for 4 issues. Single copy
price $8.99; double issue $14.99; special issue $12.99. Discount 15% on 10 to 99 copies;
20% on 100 to 499; 25% on 500 and over. Payment must accompany all orders. For foreign
subscriptions please add $9.00 for shipping and handling. Second-class postage paid at
New York, NY, and additional mailing offices. POSTMASTER: Send address changes
to HEADLINE SERIES, Foreign Policy Association, 470 Park Avenue So., New York, NY
10016. Copyright 2008 by Foreign Policy Association, Inc. Design by Agnieshka Burke.
Printed at Signature Press, Amherst Junction, Wisconsin. Published Winter 2009.

Library of Congress Control Number: 2008940049
ISBN: 978-0-87124-224-2

Introduction

TODAY, UBIQUITOUS VIOLENCE, highlighted by decapitations, torture, castrations and kidnappings carried out by drug-cartel hit men and run-of-the-mill thugs plagues Mexico. Money, revenge, ransom, extortion, access to drugs and turf battles often explain these heinous acts. On September 15, 2008, however, a major act of terrorism took place in Mexico for the first time. Around 11 p.m., as thousands of revelers celebrated Mexico's Independence Day in Morelia, a city in southwest Mexico, miscreants heaved two fragmentation grenades into the crowd. When the smoke cleared, eight people lay dead and more than 110 men, women and children were injured. TV networks beamed video footage of the

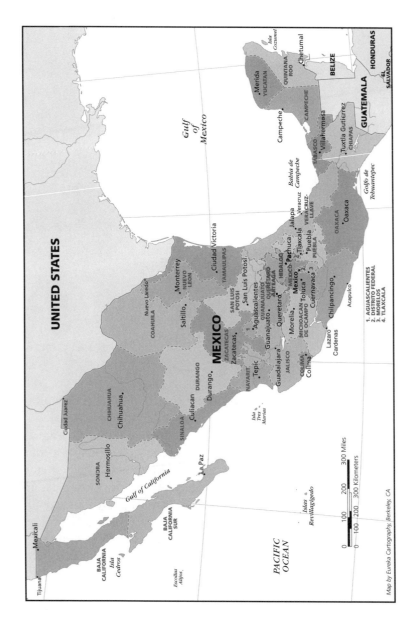

Map by Eureka Cartography, Berkeley, CA

4

blood-drenched scene to incredulous viewers across the country. Hundreds of military personnel and federal police flooded in to provide security for shocked citizens, and the Attorney General's Office (PGR) offered $1 million (10 million pesos) for information leading to the capture of the masterminds and perpetrators of the carnage. But Deputy Emilio Gamboa Patrón, owner of a supersized closet of skeletons and a big shot in the once-dominant Institutional Revolutionary party (PRI), admitted that citizens were afraid to cooperate with authorities because so many cops were allied with criminal organizations.

Meanwhile, Mexican President Felipe Calderón and other dumbfounded politicians speculated on who had inflicted the wanton slaughter amid an iconic fete in the picturesque colonial city, located in the chief executive's home state of Michoacán.

Were the perpetrators members of the powerful Gulf cartel—headquartered just below Texas in Tamaulipas state—whose ruthless paramilitary component is known as Los Zetas? Did they belong to the Gulf cartel's chief rival, the Sinaloa cartel, centered in Sinaloa state, which nestles between the Sierra Madre mountains and the Pacific Ocean? Could they be affiliated with La Familia (The Family), a shadowy, segmented gang that took credit for hanging seven banners blaming Los Zetas, three of whom were subsequently taken into custody? Might they be guerrillas either in thrall to drug mafias or launching a freelance strike?

Apart from the delinquents' identity was the ominous possibility that the attack foreshadowed an escalation in the current strife that has shaken ordinary Mexicans as well as the government: from homing in on victims to indiscriminate terrorism. The "Morelia massacre" occurred barely a week after the bloodiest day in recent memory when sadists carried out 24 executions in Mexico State alone, followed by a mutiny at Tijuana's La Mesa prison, which took the lives of at least 23 inmates while scores of convicts and guards sustained injuries.

A 'Weak' or 'Failed' State?

As never before, Mexican opinion leaders lament that their country—characterized by strong men and weak institutions—risks becoming a "failed state." For scholar Francis Fukuyama, this status denotes two dimensions of a state's powers— namely, (1) its "scope" or the different functions and goals taken on by a government and (2) its "strength" or ability to plan and execute policies. Among other things, strong states provide security, law enforcement, access to high-quality schools and health care, sound fiscal and monetary policies, responsive political systems, opportunities for employment and social mobility, retirement benefits and transparency. "Weak" states fall short in these areas; "failed" states receive F's.

Indictment of the Mexican State

Fire-breathing Cassandras are not the only ones bemoaning the conspicuous debility of the Mexican regime, but thoughtful, influential analysts as well. The pessimism extends even to those who had voiced high hopes for President Calderón, an experienced politician, a social democrat and a moderate within the center-right National Action party (PAN), who took office on December 1, 2006.

Luis Rubio, the internationally acclaimed director general of Mexico's Center of Research for Development has argued "our weaknesses as a society are formidable not only in the police and judicial domains, but also in the growing erosion of the social fabric and the absence of a sense of good and bad...."

In the same vein, Luis F. Aguilar, an astute and veteran observer, stated with respect to widespread violence: "The public insecurity exhibits the impotence of its branches of government, the futility of its laws and the incompetence of its leaders.... The tragedy is that the decomposition of the state comes from within, largely from its police whose responsibility is to apply the law fairly without exceptions…but the situation of political paralysis and institutional weakness has made us recognize that we are really a society in search for a state."

Meanwhile, Javier Hurtado, a distinguished professor at the University of Guadalajara, addressed the despair of his countrymen who took part in a massive "Light up Mexico" march on August 30, 2008, to protest the horrendous criminality and precariousness: "In the face of this situation, citizens find themselves completely vulnerable. It is neither desirable to take justice into their own hands, nor is it possible to continue to put up with inept leaders." Among the factors that buttress the weak and failed state arguments are mounting brutality, a soaring murder rate, an increase in kidnappings, the venality of local, state, and federal police forces, failure of policymakers to address hazardous conditions and disenchantment with institutions occupied by officials who live like princes even as more than one third of Mexico's 110 million people eke out a living in hardscrabble poverty. Intensifying this suffering is the toxic spillover from America's subprime lending crisis, falling oil prices and a nosedive in remittances to Mexico from friends and family members in the United States.

The 'Colombianization' of Mexico?

In describing the surging drug violence along the U.S.-Mexican border and elsewhere in Mexico, law enforcement officials and analysts increasingly refer to Colombia, where the Medellín drug cartel and other criminal organizations waged war on the government and killed hundreds of people during the 1980s.

An analyst at the libertarian Cato Institute wrote that "Mexico is a major source of heroin, marijuana, and methamphetamine for the United States as well as the principal transit and distribution point for cocaine coming in from South America…. There are growing signs that the Colombianization of Mexico is now becoming a reality." "The violence of cartels has acquired another dimension: now executions are public..., their messages are no longer coded but are also open in order to generate doubt and fear," commented Jorge Fernández Menéndez, a Mexican security expert.

However, Colombia's government has neither enjoyed the legitimacy of its Mexican counterpart nor exercised control over vast areas of the country. Yet the Mexican cartels exercise dominance over certain zones: areas of the Tierra Caliente, a fertile mountainous area contiguous to Michoacán, Guerrero and Mexico State; the "Golden Triangle," a drug-producing mecca at the intersection of the states of Sinaloa, Chihuahua and Durango in the Sierra Madres; the Isthmus of Tehuantepec in the southeast; and sectors along the U.S.-Mexican border where cartel thugs carve up judges, police officers and journalists who incur their wrath. The government has traditionally maintained a presence in most of the nation, chiefly through the army. However, even military commanders now worry about losing sovereignty to these merchants of death.

This HEADLINE SERIES will examine Mexican President Calderón's initiatives in battling the criminal syndicates and consider their impact on the United States, where they increasingly conduct their nefarious ventures. But first, how did "drugs and thugs" become such a powerful force? And how did Mexico arrive at this perilous crossroad?

1

Wars and the Spread of Drugs

Wars have spurred the production, processing and transport of drugs, as well as their consumption, in both Mexico and the United States. Raw opium was highly regarded well before the birth of Christ. However, it was not until 1805 that scientists finally refined the "miracle drug" morphine from opium. Combatants in the Mexican-American War (1846–48) smoked marijuana, which was legal in both nations. In 1853 two American physicians first used a hypodermic needle to inject morphine directly into the blood system. During the U.S. Civil War, Confederate and Union doctors prescribed morphine and other narcotics not only to abate suffering from wounds and operations, but also to treat malaria, dysentery and diarrhea. Elaine

Shannon, author of *Desperados* (1988), observed that morphine addiction was so pronounced that it was called "the army disease." Some raised the alarm about this dependence after hostilities concluded, and often the response was to substitute it with another drug.

Throughout the nineteenth century, pharmacies in both nations sold over-the-counter nostrums that contained narcotics, as well as regularly prescribed medications like laudanum and paregoric. The Sears catalog even touted a morphine-laced mixture that could be slipped into a wayward spouse's coffee to keep him home at night.

In the United States, a year after Atlanta's Fulton County enacted Prohibition in 1885, Dr. John Stith Pemberton invented Coca-Cola, a carbonated, nonalcoholic beverage flavored with kola nut and containing a small portion of cocaine. In 1898, the Bayer Company began marketing a nonaddictive cough suppressant for children named "heroin," derived from the word *heroisch*, German for powerful, which it certainly proved to be— eight times more so than morphine. As with aspirin, Bayer lost its trademark rights to heroin following the defeat of Germany in World War I.

In 1906 the Chinese government spearheaded a campaign against opium use to spur modernization and attenuate the influence of Western imperialism. Anger at the mistreatment of Chinese nationals in the United States precipitated a voluntary boycott of American products by the regime in Peking (now Beijing). President Theodore Roosevelt (1901–09) sought to propitiate the Chinese by supporting their antiopium venture. Washington participated actively in the 13-nation International Opium Commission, which held conferences in Shanghai (1909) and The Hague (1911). The latter approved a convention whose signatories agreed to suppress opiates and limit narcotics to medical use. Thus began U.S. efforts at controlling worldwide narcotics traffic, which continue today.

The collapse of Porfirio Díaz's protracted dictatorship in 1911 sparked the Mexican Revolution, which found soldiers spreading the marijuana habit throughout the country. The national ban on the cultivation and marketing of marijuana (1920) and opium poppy (1926) occurred amid simmering unrest, which was finally contained by the creation of a dominant single party in 1929—the forerunner of today's Institutional Revolutionary party.

Origins of the U.S. War on Drugs

In the late nineteenth and early twentieth centuries, the Anti-Saloon League (ASL) and the Women's Christian Temperance Union (WCTU) formed part of a crazy-quilt coalition in the United States that encompassed pietistic Protestants in the Democratic and Republican parties, most women, African-American leaders and Progressives. The ASL looked forward to "an era of clear thinking and clean living." The Progressive Movement emerged to improve the quality of life and invigorate the nation's moral fiber by preserving the environment, stanching the use of mood-altering substances and halting the sale of adulterated foods. One of its first victories came with the passage of the Pure Food and Drug Act in 1906. This measure did not prevent the sale of narcotics, but it did mandate accurate labeling of all patent medicines sold in interstate commerce.

Although some states imposed bans, it was not until the entry of the United States into World War I that "drys" obtained enactment of national legislation. WWI invested Prohibition with a patriotic aura, since German-Americans owned many breweries. Once the United States declared war in April 1917, Congress mandated liquor-free zones around military camps. Eight months later, Congress passed the 18th Amendment, ushering in Prohibition.

Although conceived to reduce alcoholism, promote family unity and curtail absenteeism, Prohibition had unintended consequences. "Speakeasies," or clandestine watering holes, flourished. Organized crime swooped into this illegal but profitable business. Chicago's Al "Scarface" Capone and his nemesis George "Bugs" Moran made fortunes through bootlegging even as gun-toting federal agents smashed stills and raided warehouses across the country. The sharp increase in smuggling and violent crime spurred repeal of what President Herbert Hoover (1929–33) had called "a noble experiment" in 1933, after Democrat Franklin D. Roosevelt had swept him from office at the depth of the Great Depression.

At the same time in Mexico, a famous drug trafficker, Enrique Fernández, became known as the "Al Capone of Ciudad Juárez"—across the Rio Grande from El Paso—because of his ostentatious wealth and clout with government officials. Governors of the Northern District of Baja California—then a territory—not only imposed tariffs on the Chinese who shipped opium from Sinaloa via Tijuana to San Francisco, they also got rich from the promotion of gambling, prostitution and the manufacture, sale and export of alcoholic beverages. Hollywood celebrities and even Capone frequented casinos and clubs in Tijuana and Mexicali, the main portals for illegal substances flowing into the United States from the 1930s to the 1950s. Meanwhile, María Dolores Estévez, known as "Lola la Chata," was the salient drug figure in Mexico City, where opium dens catered to the elite.

Marijuana and poppy flourished in the remote Sinaloan municipalities, as well as in the neighboring states of Durango and Chihuahua. In the beginning, these substances represented normal crops grown by local farmers. *Gomeros*, or gum makers, converted the poppy into opium paste for sale, and a "live-and-let-live" ethos enveloped these activities. After World War II, the press in Culiacán, the capital of Sinaloa state, even urged the government to seek UN permission to legalize poppy production as was done in Yugoslavia, India, Turkey and Iran—to generate work and income for local residents.

Prohibition had fostered the rise and consolidation of organized crime in Mexico as "rumrunners" prospered during the 1920s and early 1930s. That experience further prepared them to engage in the drug trade, beginning in the 1940s. In the late 1950s, Culiacán—described as the "opium smugglers' base of operations"—became the situs for an underground economy based on narcotics destined for the United States. The state's long coastline, the completion of the Pan-American Highway and the construction of a regional airport in the 1960s facilitated

Beer barrels are destroyed by Prohibition agents in an unknown location on January 16, 1920. (AP Photo)

a network that enabled the Sinaloa cartel to gain hegemony in Mexico's Pacific northwest. Badiraguato, a mountainous municipality in Sinaloa, near its intersection with the states of Durango and Chihuahua, earned sobriquets as "opium central" and the "hideout for hundreds of hoodlums."

In the late 1930s, President Lázaro Cárdenas (1934–40) ordered the military to destroy marijuana and poppy crops in Sinaloa. The state's governor, Colonel Rodolfo T. Loaiza (1941–44), proposed "exterminating narcotics trafficking" and converting drug-cultivating farms in the municipalities of Badiraguato and nearby Mocorito into bean and corn producers. In February 1944, the state executive was murdered, apparently on the orders of former War and Navy Secretary Pablo Macías Valenzuela, who ascended to the governorship.

Four years after the repeal of Prohibition, Harry J. Anslinger, the crusading chief of the Federal Bureau of Narcotics (FBN), spearheaded another social experiment when he convinced Congress to pass the Marijuana Tax Act of 1937. The FBN zealot argued that cannabis caused "murder, insanity and death." In 1969 the Supreme Court struck down the law as violative of the Fifth Amendment inasmuch as anyone seeking the tax stamp would have to incriminate himself.

Unlike opiates and cocaine, the introduction of marijuana came during a period of drug intolerance. The practice of smoking cannabis arrived in the United States with Mexican immigrants who had come North during the 1920s to work, and it soon caught the fancy of jazz musicians. Widespread use did not take place until the 1960s, 40 years after marijuana cigarettes had reached America.

World War II

Japan's occupation of poppy-producing regions in Asia, combined with Turkey's alliance with the Axis powers, forced

Washington informally to seek an alternative source of opium to produce morphine during World War II. Enrique Diarte reigned over the opium trade in Tijuana and Mexicali until Max Cossman reportedly had him executed in 1944. Known as the "king of opium," Cossman forged links to Mickey Cohen of the old Al Capone gang. Fellow Americans Bugsy Siegel, who was linked to the Charles "Lucky" Luciano and Meyer Lansky mobs, and his girlfriend, Virginia Hill, connived with local politicians to grow poppies in Mexico's northwest.

For decades, Mexican-based traffickers had produced and smuggled drugs. During World War II, however, Mexico became a source of morphine for the legal market and heroin for the illegal trade. The war also swelled the demand for hemp fiber for rope, which led to large-scale cultivation of marijuana in both Mexico and the United States. Ernesto "Don Neto" Fonseca Carrillo, known as "the Godfather," pioneered extensive poppy production and trade. He also served as mentor to Rafael Caro Quintero, a shrewd and youthful entrepreneur who converted Mexican marijuana from second-rate weed to the choice of aficionados by perfecting a seedless variety of the plant *(sinsemilla)*. In the postwar years, Sinaloans held sway over the business, beginning with opium smuggling and, depending on demand, gradually branching into marijuana, cocaine and methamphetamines. Growth in consumption eventually led to the formation of a more cohesive organization in the 1970s.

Once the Allies had won, the United States resumed importing superior opium for medicinal purposes from Asia and the Middle East. Still, Mexico continued to remain a source of narcotics, especially when tens of thousands of service personnel returned from overseas with a taste for, if not an addiction to, drugs. Washington again pressured the Mexican regime to curb the export of controlled substances.

Before the 1940s, governors of producing and trafficking

states had the power to regulate unlawful business in their territories. In 1947, President Miguel Alemán (1946–52) created the Federal Security Directorate (DFS), which worked with the Attorney General's Office, its Federal Judicial Police (PJF) and the army to combat forbidden commerce. Civilians and military officials who had direct responsibility for fighting traffickers often became the institutional mediators between criminals and the power structure. Neither mediators nor traffickers boasted free reign: they were both subordinate to political power centered in state executives, who—in turn—answered to the president and his lieutenants.

Although concentrating on radicals, guerrillas and "cold war" subversives, the ruthless DFS maintained authority over other law-enforcement agencies, as well as responsibility for investigating drug-related operations. The American embassy's military attaché compared the force to the Gestapo in light of its vast powers, fondness for torture and the questionable backgrounds of its leaders. Alemán, whose term was tarnished by corruption, engaged in investment with American underworld figures after leaving office and "probably his most lasting legacy was a reputation for graft and corruption on a scale heretofore unknown in Mexico."

After World War II, authorities on both sides of the border extolled the "special relationship" between their countries. American investment poured into Mexico to take advantage of incentives embedded in Mexico's import-substitution scheme; bilateral trade flourished, thanks to a steady peso-dollar exchange rate; Mexican leaders spurned communism; and despite growing commerce in opiates and marijuana since the late 1940s, the question of drugs garnered scant attention at bilateral meetings. Mexico was beginning a 25-year period of robust growth, formidable industrialization and political stability under authoritarian PRI regimes.

Operation Intercept

This era of good feelings changed when President Richard M. Nixon (1969–74) took office. He faced an upswing in drug consumption, especially marijuana, because of the permissiveness of the "hippie" years of the 1960s. This situation coincided with rising heroin dependency among Vietnam conflict (1959–75) veterans. The boom in demand for controlled substances sparked a surge in cultivation and riches south of the border.

Although he had run on a muscular law-and-order platform, once in office Nixon found that the federal government had little enforcement power against violent felonies. Thus, the new chief executive established the Presidential Task Force Relating to Narcotics, Marijuana and Dangerous Drugs. This body set as its highest priority "an eradication of the production and refinement in Mexico of opium poppies and marijuana."

Their report pointed to Mexico as a crucial source of heroin and identified marijuana as a critical "stepping-stone" to heroin addiction. The White House claimed that abusers committed serious crimes and vowed to block the influx of narcotics. When Washington urged the spraying of drug fields with the herbicide Paraquat, Mexican authorities—using diplomatic language—told U.S. officials, in effect, "to go piss up a rope," according to Nixon aide G. Gordon Liddy, who had been involved in the initiative.

Nixon responded with "Operation Intercept," which began in September 1969 and entailed some 2,000 customs and border patrol agents meticulously examining vehicles, shoppers and workers crossing into Mexico. Simultaneously, the U.S. Army stationed mobile radar units from El Paso to San Diego to impede northbound flights of marijuana-laden aircraft. The two-week logjam of cars, trucks and pedestrians in this "nightmarish dragnet" wreaked economic chaos in the border zone.

To break the impasse, Mexico City begrudgingly unveiled

"Operation Cooperation." In return for allowing American law-enforcement agents to monitor Mexican poppy and marijuana fields, Mexican soldiers began hacking away at drug plants with machetes. Aerial spraying had yet to be introduced and the joint effort proved futile. As U.S. Drug Enforcement Administration (DEA) agent Jaime Kuykendall later said: "The traffickers got the message for a little while that we were serious.... But it didn't last. We quit showing them we're serious, so they figured everything was hunky-dory." Operation Intercept benefited powerful criminals who used swift boats and small planes at the expense of amateurs who could not survive without the ready cash derived from overland trafficking.

The failure of interdiction aside, Nixon signed into law the Controlled Substances Act (CSA) of 1970. This measure laid the foundation for the current "War on Drugs." Congress placed

Gigantic traffic jams at the U.S. border with Mexico in 1969 resulted from 'Operation Intercept,' a campaign by President Richard M. Nixon to stop the smuggling of narcotics and marijuana. (AP Photo)

the burden of enforcement on the Bureau of Narcotics and Dangerous Drugs and the President retooled his strategy as a "total war" on heroin and a "crusade to save our children."

In 1973 Congress created the DEA as an entity with prime responsibility for narcotic matters. The previous year, authorities had thwarted the transit of high-quality morphine paste from Marseille to New York—the "French Connection" celebrated in the eponymous film. This stroke transformed heroin market and distribution patterns, giving impetus to the expanded cultivation of opium poppy in Mexico. Demand escalated for "Mexican mud," or brown heroin, and from 1972 through 1976, Mexican mafiosi controlled three fourths of the U.S. heroin market while still satisfying Americans' appetite for marijuana.

During the PRI's heyday before the presidency of Ernesto Zedillo (1994–2000), high-level federal authorities controlled drug kingpins. The latter often anteed up $250,000 simply to meet with representatives of federal and state executives to attain protection from the police forces that operated in the country. Some generals also received hefty payoffs for their cooperation. In this environment, PRI governors worked through state and local enforcement chiefs and PRI politicians to allocate *"plazas"*—areas and corridors where the gangs held sway to produce, store or ship drugs—often charging 10 percent less than federal authorities. They followed a "1-2-3 System": a payoff to authorities of $1 million for an interior location; $2 million for a coastal zone; and $3 million for a U.S.-Mexico border crossing. In return for generous bribes, *mordidas,* the desperados pursued their illicit activities with the connivance of authorities and in accord with mutually understood "rules of the game." In Sinaloa, the production of poppy and marijuana began as a family enterprise passed down from one generation to another, with Badiraguato gaining fame as the cynosure of output and the bailiwick of many capos (crime syndicate heads).

Any clashes that occurred among families or between traffickers and police took place in "Mi Delirio," "Montecarlo" and other bars in the rough-and-tumble Tierra Blanca neighborhood of Culiacán. Analyst Leo Zuckermann notes that officials tolerated robberies but not kidnappings; and the criminals could engage in growing, processing and trafficking but not in homicides, least of all the murder of civilians. Execution of focs and the sale of drugs should be accomplished north of the border. The drug dons acted with civility toward authorities, appeared with governors at their children's weddings and baptisms, and knew they would suffer deadly consequences if they violated the "live-and-let-live" ethos.

Gradually, the prospect of fattening one's bank account by selling heroin and marijuana altered the informal rules of the game between lawbreakers and presumed law enforcers, beginning in Sinaloa. In 1957 the federal police boasted superior firepower over the cartels, whose operatives relied on handguns. A decade later, the drug rings had acquired high-powered weapons, had started assailing each other and had even begun killing policemen—with some shoot-outs taking place in populous areas. Nevertheless, the government still held the whip even though its hand had begun to shake. No semblance of such an authoritarian control mechanism exists today in most of Mexico, where fragmentation of power has become the norm.

An eruption of violence in the 1970s incurred the ire of President José López Portillo (1976–82), who launched "Operation Condor"—a follow-up to Operation Cooperation—soon after taking office. This measure involved tens of thousands of soldiers headed by General José Hernández Toledo and concentrated on defoliating illegal plantations in the mountains of Sinaloa, Durango and Chihuahua. As a result, reports of human-rights abuses proliferated. This intense campaign drove traffickers to Guadalajara, a virtual "sanctuary city" where the drug lords and their families lived quietly while transferring their unlawful activities to Nayarit, Colima and Michoacán, in what is termed the "cucaracha effect."

The War on Terrorism

In the new millennium, the conflict against illegal substances took on a different dimension. After the 9/11 terrorist attacks, the DEA sought a role in President George W. Bush's "war on terrorism" to justify more money and additional responsibility. In 2004, DEA administrator Karen P. Tandy told Congress that opium production in Afghanistan "is a significant concern and a priority for the DEA because of its im-

April 26, 2002: Afghan farmers harvest opium poppies near the eastern Afghan town of Ghani Khiel, home to Afghanistan's biggest drug market. Farmers who voluntarily destroyed their crops were supposed to get $500. Instead they got a chit verifying they had destroyed their crops and then were turned away when they tried to collect their money. (AP Photo/Amir Shah)

pact on worldwide drug supply and its potential…to provide financial support to terrorists and other destabilizing groups."

Two years earlier, Tandy had backed "Operation Containment" to make a "concerted effort" to coordinate activities among 19 countries in Central Asia, the Caucasus, Europe and Russia. Its aim was to "deprive drug-trafficking organizations of their market access and international terrorist groups of financial support from drugs, precursor chemicals, weapons, ammunition and currency." The DEA had reopened its Kabul Country Office in February 2003, and reportedly made "superb contributions under these difficult circumstances" in gathering and disseminating intelligence to United States and British law-enforcement agencies, while supporting the Pentagon's creation of a "fusion center" for multinational information sharing.

Meanwhile, the DEA enlarged its presence in Europe and Southwest Asia, opened a new office in Uzbekistan and assigned special agents to its Kabul, Ankara, Istanbul, Tashkent, Moscow and London offices. While concentrating on the Middle East, the DEA raised the specter that terrorists and Mexican smugglers worked jointly. The agency cited contacts between Mexican traffickers and guerrillas of the Revolutionary Armed Forces of Colombia (FARC).

2

The Weakening of the Mexican State

Some specialists have traced the decline of the PRI-dominated government to the 1968 Tlatelolco Massacre, when police and soldiers shot and killed hundreds of student and middle-class demonstrators. Others have charged the erratic policies of President Luis Echeverría Álvarez (1970–76) with impelling the state's enervation. He ran up distended budget deficits, sharply increased government intervention in the economy, alienated the "Monterrey Group" of conservative northern industrialists, oversaw a "dirty war" waged by the Brigada Blanca (White Bri-

For details on cartels, drug lords, and structure of Mexican government anti-drug operations see appendices beginning on page 68.

gade) against dissidents and crossed swords with Washington over his strident advocacy of the affluent First World's distribution of resources to the impecunious Third World.

Echeverría's regime concluded with an economic crisis, which forced the devaluation of the peso and subsequent belt-tightening recommended by the International Monetary Fund (IMF), a bête noire for populists like the lame-duck Mexican chief of state. The nation's economic woes escalated under López Portillo, who mismanaged newly discovered oil reserves, borrowed billions of dollars abroad and presided over an orgy of corruption. The fall in petroleum prices forced the arrogant national leader to submit to a burdensome rescue plan crafted by the United States, the IMF and other foreign lenders. As a gesture of defiance, López Portillo took advantage of his farewell State of the Nation address, delivered on September 1, 1982, to nationalize the country's banking system. This daredevil move made the state a shareholder in hundreds of corporations and sparked distrust between the business community and the government, which had enjoyed a long history of cooperative enrichment. As one insider noted, "In the past we had fought like cats and dogs during the day only to sleep together at night."

The next chief executive, Miguel de la Madrid Hurtado (1982–88), had run on a "Moral Renovation" platform, vowing to combat malfeasance and hold fair contests. When the center-right National Action party began winning local elections in the north, PRI dinosaurs egregiously manipulated the 1986 gubernatorial contest in Chihuahua. This move excited large demonstrations by supporters of the "losing" PAN nominee.

The government suffered another black eye on May 30, 1984, when killers gunned down Manuel Buendía, the nation's leading syndicated columnist, in the heart of Mexico City. The 58-year-old journalist's feisty front-page commentary in the *Excelsior* newspaper had frequently exposed dishonesty and deceit in the upper tiers of officialdom, labor and the corporate world. Buendía's death did not halt muckraking. In mid-1985, the weekly magazine *Proceso* publicized the criminal activities of DFS Director José Antonio Zorrilla Pérez, who, eight years later, was convicted along with four others for Buendía's murder and sentenced to 35 years in prison.

On September 19, 1985, "a mighty blow from hell" struck Mexico City in an earthquake that registered 7.8 on the Richter scale; a second major tremor assailed the capital area on the following day. De la Madrid's vacillation in responding to this disaster cost the PRI dearly, particularly in the Federal District's devastated 13-square-mile central zone. It undermined the legitimacy of the chief executive and the single-party apparatus over which he presided. The paternalistic regime failed to take care of its people in their greatest moment of need and the PRI's approval level plunged. In the wake of a disaster that resulted in some 10,000 deaths and left tens of thousands homeless, any ward politician worth his patronage allotment would have clamped on a hard hat, rolled up his sleeves and waded into the smoking debris. Yet as average Mexicans organized to rescue family members, neighbors and fellow workers, one diplomat noted that de la Madrid appeared as more of an "accountant scrutinizing a balance sheet" than as the concerned patriarch of a tormented national family. The "vaunted organizational talents of the PRI were nowhere in evidence" and "the party's labor and agrarian wings, which on numerous occasions had convoked hundreds of thousands of trade unionists and peasants for political rallies, failed to mobilize anybody to aid the earthquake victims."

De la Madrid's team of colorless technocrats lacked either popularity or well-cultivated rapport with the people, and many of the "old guard" proved incompetent. Police extracted bribes from victims who wanted to cross security lines and search for loved ones. The capital's residents had to cope with the crisis with minimal official help. Taxis became ambulances, ham-radio operators configured a communications network and agile young people—known as "moles"—dug with their hands in the rubble of collapsed buildings to locate victims. "We realized for the first time that we could help each other without relying on the government," recalled a community activist.

The Government and Criminals

The influence of criminal organizations expanded as the regime became weaker and the social fabric began to unravel. The "no-reelection" article in the Mexican constitution brought a new chief executive and his security entourage to power every six years. This provision sometimes changed the ascendancy—or even the ability to do business—of multibillion-dollar cartels. In fact, Mexican administrations that went on the offensive knew the futility of trying to attack all of the gangs at the same time. Still, as the prospects for accumulating vast sums of narco-dollars brightened, most of the bosses retained their plazas long enough to retire in affluence beyond the dreams of a Medici prince. A change in gubernatorial roles attended the ascent to power of PAN state leaders, most of whom refused to work hand-in-glove with underworld figures. This watershed was preceded by an acrimonious conflict between Mexico and the United States over the death of a DEA agent.

Camarena Case

Six months before the 1985 Mexico City earthquakes, the brutal torture and execution of DEA agent Enrique "Kiki" Camarena Salazar dominated headlines on both sides of the border. From Washington's perspective, the incident converted narcotics smuggling from a law-enforcement issue to one of national security. On March 6, 1985, authorities discovered the decomposed bodies of Camarena and his Mexican pilot

Enrique Camarena Salazar,
award-winning undercover agent for
the U.S. Drug Enforcement Agency,
who was murdered brutally
in Mexico in 1985.
(AP Photo)

swathed in plastic bags and buried 70 miles south of Guadalajara. Prosecutors believed the murders constituted retaliation for a series of drug raids that had cost the capos billions of dollars.

Camarena was working on "Operation Godfather," investigating Miguel Ángel Félix Gallardo, the drug boss who supplied heroin and cocaine to southern California and other Sun Belt areas. Félix Gallardo rapidly built a structure that stretched from the Andes to major U.S. cities; he shipped a ton and a half to two tons of cocaine each month, which put him on a par with Medellín's notorious drug barons. A high-school football star and ex-marine, Camarena had incurred the wrath of kingpins Félix Gallardo and Rafael Caro Quintero by exposing large irrigated marijuana farms in Chihuahua that had flourished with the connivance of federal authorities, local police and the army.

Foot-dragging by Mexican officials investigating the slaughter infuriated residents of Camarena's hometown of Calexico, California, where the population is overwhelmingly Mexican-American. Along the major highway, local citizens erected a billboard that proclaimed: "Warning: Not Safe to Travel to Guadalajara, Mexico." Meanwhile, U.S. customs agents displayed their anger by meticulously searching vehicles at the frontier, virtually paralyzing border traffic for several days.

American officials accused their Mexican counterparts of allowing Camarena's assassins to escape. Some Mexican law-enforcement agents insisted that the torture of the swashbuckling DEA operative betokened his complicity in shady dealings with drug lords he had double-crossed. They also claimed that the DEA, whose reputation paled in comparison with that of the Federal Bureau of Investigation and Central Intelligence Agency, was seeking a hero to burnish its image.

Authorities eventually hunted down Caro Quintero in Costa Rica and in 1989 he was sentenced to 40 years in prison for the murder of a man who became a martyr among fellow DEA agents. When lawyers employed a technicality to overturn this conviction, the Mexican Attorney General's Office insisted that Caro Quintero would not be freed because he was already behind bars for another crime. In the unlikely event that Caro Quintero overturns his Mexican sentences, there is a long-standing request on file for his arrest and extradition to the United States, according to a U.S. Justice Department official who spoke on condition of anonymity.

Legal maneuvering infuriated Camarena's former fellow agents. "Kiki's killing symbolized corruption at its worst in Mexico," said Philip Jordan, a retired DEA special agent in Dallas and former director of the El Paso Intelligence Center. "We know why Kiki was taken from us—because the [Mexican] government was working in complicity with the godfathers of the drug trade...." Camarena's execution reverberated throughout Washington and poisoned U.S.-Mexican relations for years.

The DEA's forcible abduction from Guadalajara of a Mexican physician believed to have been implicated in the Camarena affair exacerbated bilateral tensions as Washington laid plans to "militarize" the fight against illegal substances. Dr. Humberto Álvarez Machain, whom U.S. authorities had snared with bounty hunters, was ultimately acquitted by the U.S. District Court in Los Angeles.

This policy found expression in the National Defense Authorization Act of 1989, designating the Pentagon as the "single lead agency" for the detection and monitoring of illicit drug shipments into the United States. Soon thereafter, President George H.W. Bush (1989–93) announced his Andean Initiative, a $2.2 billion, five-year plan aimed at stopping the cocaine trade at its source. Although U.S. military personnel had been involved in training, equipping and transporting foreign antinarcotics personnel since the early 1980s, the Andean strategy dramatically enlarged their role and expanded the infusion of U.S. assistance into the police and military forces. Bolivia and Peru, the world's two other major coca-producing nations, also received sharp increases in assistance, but the majority of the drug-war funds went to Colombia. In 1989 Colombia got $18 million for military and police assistance. A year later, U.S. funding to Colombia increased fivefold, making it the Western Hemisphere's number one recipient of U.S. security assistance, a distinction it maintains today. At the same time, the Pentagon devoted additional resources to detecting and monitoring operations in the Caribbean and the Gulf of Mexico. The heightened surveillance prompted Colombian dons to divert cocaine and heroin shipments through Central America and via the Pacific Ocean, with both routes leading ominously through Mexico. Continual attacks on the Cali and Medellín operations forced these cartels to reorganize into smaller units to minimize penetration and carry on operations. The fragmentation of erstwhile Colombian leviathans opened the way for ever-wealthier Mexican cartels to morph from carriers to purchasers of cocaine, which they sold in the U.S. market.

The Certification Process

In reaction to the Camarena case, U.S. legislators passed the Anti-Drug Abuse Act of 1986, which required the President to make yearly determinations—and report to Congress—on the progress of drug-producing and/or drug-transit countries' efforts to eliminate the drug threat. Washington would slash by 50 percent its foreign aid to decertified nations and oppose their loan applications in the IMF, the World Bank and other international agencies. Only counternarcotics and humanitarian aid would be available for "decertified" nations.

As part of the certification process, the U.S. Department of State's Bureau of International Narcotics and Law Enforcement Affairs presented findings on drug strategies and policies, as well as current drug trafficking and abuse situations in every nation listed as a major drug-producing and/or drug-transit country, precursor chemical–source or money-laundering state. In theory, this report provided an objective basis for determining compliance with U.S. law and, at the same time, publicized the status of the countries evaluated. In fact, it spawned a diplomatic nightmare.

As a former envoy observed: "The annual narcotics certification drama dominated U.S.-Mexican relations for years, causing untold grief for successive ambassadors and always roiling the bilateral waters. By 1998, certification was an idea that had outlived whatever usefulness it might have ever had." Although the United States never blacklisted Mexico, Colombia, which appeared immobilized by the rise and consolidation of the Medellín and Cali cartels, suffered decertification in 1996 and 1997. In retaliation, Colombian President Ernest Samper (1994–98) suspended eradication flights over coca- and poppy-growing zones. In 2001, Senator Kay Bailey Hutchison of Texas (R) introduced legislation that suspended the annual certification process with Mexico for a year in hope of improving bilateral cooperation. While an attenuated version remains on the books, the decertification statute has become a dead letter with respect to Mexico.

Congress passed the Anti-Drug Abuse Act of 1988 to create the Office of National Drug Control Policy (ONDCP) within the executive branch. The ONDCP establishes policies, priorities and objectives for the nation's drug-control program, with a view to reducing illicit drug use, manufacturing and trafficking, drug-related crime and violence and drug-related health consequences.

Although Mexico produces a small percentage of the global supply of opium poppy, its growers and processors have furnished a robust share of the heroin distributed in the United States thanks to imports from Colombia and other South American nations. Furthermore, Mexico has for decades stood out as the largest foreign distributor of marijuana to its northern neighbor, as well as the top producer and supplier of methamphetamine and other "designer drugs," giving rise to a $35-billion-a-year drug trade.

In late 1993, President Bill Clinton (1993–2001) pledged to move from the failed supply-side strategy toward "a comprehensive national crusade against drug abuse" and associated violence and lawbreaking at home. He shifted from emphasizing transit interdiction to encouraging source countries to build institutions, destroy trafficking gangs and stanch supplies of illicit drugs. Authorities apprehended the head honchos of the Medellín and Cali cartels. Clinton also invoked the International Emergency Economic Powers Act to freeze their assets in the United States in addition to barring Americans from doing business with them. Moreover, Clinton sought to dismantle the "air bridge" that connected coca growers and coca paste manufacturers in Peru and Bolivia with Colombian refiners and distributors. As a result, exporters quickly abandoned air routes in favor of the region's labyrinth of waterways. The Pentagon responded by supporting initiatives that targeted the sea routes in both source countries and their neighbors.

President Carlos Salinas de Gortari (1988–94) was eager to propitiate Washington. He knew that narco-violence and ubiquitous venality could block the North American Free Trade Agreement (NAFTA, 1994) that he so enthusiastically championed. During a mid-1990 trip to the United States, the Mexican leader agreed to admit armed DEA agents into Mexico, as well as permit the deployment of satellites to detect drug operations.

To demonstrate his commitment, the Mexican leader established a Center for Drug Control Planning (CENDRO), which carried out intelligence functions; the National Drug Control Program; and the National Institute to Combat Drugs, under the jurisdiction of the Attorney General's Office. One of the most bizarre events during Salinas's term was the May 24, 1993, daylight murder of Cardinal Juan Jesús Posadas Ocampo at the Guadalajara airport. Hit men from the Tijuana cartel fired 14 bullets into the cleric's body, apparently mistaking him for a rival drug lord who also rode in a swanky black limousine.

After the assassination of Luis Donaldo Colosio, the PRI's first presidential candidate for the 1994 election, Salinas selected Ernesto Zedillo, a Yale-trained Ph.D. economist, to succeed him. The "December crisis" later that year exploded three weeks after the new chief executive's inauguration and quickly turned into the worst economic nightmare since the Great Depression. A first-rate economist but a green-as-grass politician, the brainy leader devoted himself to righting the convulsed economy. However, the debilitation of the Mexican state soon became obvious.

Zedillo, who lacked a political base, infuriated PRI big shots by meeting with the PAN, the leftist-nationalist Democratic

Revolution party (PRD) and smaller parties as he sought to resolve the crisis bequeathed to him. To his credit, he ordered the incarceration of the ex-president's brother, Raúl Salinas, on charges of illegally enriching himself and murdering his brother-in-law. Nonetheless, the president's lack of strength became clear-cut when he could not prevent PRI stalwart, Roberto Madrazo Pintado, from assuming the governorship of Tabasco in the aftermath of a fraud-drenched election in 1994. Twelve years later, Madrazo lost the presidential race to Calderón.

Zedillo did send Gulf cartel leader Juan García Abrego to the

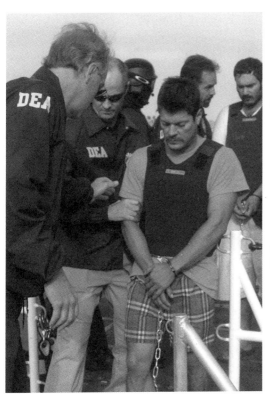

Mexican drug king-pin Francisco Javier Arellano Félix, in DEA custody as he arrives in San Diego, California, on Aug. 17, 2006. The head of Mexico's largest family-run cartel, which controlled much of the western Mexico-U.S. border drug trade, received a mandatory life sentence in a plea agreement, which came after prosecutors agreed not to seek the death penalty. (AP Photo/Department of Justice)

United States rather than turn him over to the Mexican judicial system. Worst of all was the revelation that the president's drug czar, General Jesús Gutiérrez Rebollo—whom his U.S. counterpart General Barry McCaffrey had vouchsafed as "a guy of absolute, unquestioned integrity" —was on the payroll of the Chihuahua-based Juárez cartel.

In May 1998 the Mexican state suffered another shock with the revelation of "Operation Casablanca," a three-year U.S. undercover investigation in which U.S. Customs Service agents examined major Mexican banking institutions for laundering tainted drug profits. The sting spurred the arrest of 22 high-ranking and mid-level bankers from a dozen of Mexico's 19 largest banks. In addition, authorities seized $35 million in illegal proceeds, two tons of cocaine and four tons of marijuana. "By infiltrating the highest levels of the international drug-trafficking financial infrastructure, customs was able to crack the elaborate financial schemes the drug traffickers developed to launder the tremendous volumes of cash acquired as proceeds from their deadly trade," U.S. Treasury Secretary Robert Rubin announced.

The Americans did not even notify Zedillo of the maneuver, which he lambasted as a breach of "sovereignty." Even as it defended the raid against the money launderers, the White House tried to mollify the irate Mexicans. In a phone call to Zedillo, Clinton "expressed regret that better prior consultation had not been possible in this case." U.S. officials said they did not alert the Mexicans because they feared for the safety of the undercover agents. A number of Mexican officials were believed to be involved in drug trafficking themselves and a leak might have frustrated the scheme.

Voters got their revenge for the economic debacle of the mid-1990s by depriving the PRI of its majority in Congress (1997), placing PRD luminary Cuauhtémoc Cárdenas in the Mexico

City mayor's office (1997) and electing several opposition governors (late 1990s). In 2000 the unthinkable happened as the PRI lost the presidency to which its leaders thought they had a birthright, thus signaling the end of their party's hegemony.

The unwillingness of supposedly clean PAN governors, who did not comprehend the traditional rules of the game, to take bribes in return for acquiescing to narco-activities found the drug lords suborning state and local law-enforcement officials without the control mechanisms that PRI officials had exercised. Thus, narco-violence began to climb under PAN state executives in Baja California (Ernesto Ruffo Appel/1989–95) and Chihuahua (Francisco Barrio Terrazas/1992–98), states that remain hotbeds of insecurity. As Luis Rubio has observed, "In the security realm, decentralization of power had spurred the feudalization of the country and, with it, the growth of crime."

The ineptness of Vicente Fox Quesada (2000–2006), the first PAN president, who took office on December 1, 2000, further debilitated the state. A superb vote winner, but a hapless politician, Fox failed to unite his National Action party behind his ever-changing program. He tried to ingratiate himself with the Zapatista National Liberation Army, but the Chiapas-based rebels scorned his overtures. He even abandoned a plan to construct a new airport for Mexico City—the "centerpiece" of his public works agenda—when machete-waving dissidents decried the project.

Fox's vulnerability became evident in April 2002 when he sought permission to visit briefly Canada and the United States. For the first time in history, Congress denied a president's request to leave the country; Fox had become a lame duck with four years left in his term.

Meanwhile, inter-cartel violence escalated in Michoacán during Fox's years. The Sinaloa cartel encroached on the domain of the Tamaulipas-based Gulf cartel, headed by Osiel Cárdenas

Guillén. Cárdenas Guillén counterattacked by sending Los Zetas to seize transit routes through Michoacán, whose ports serve as arrival points for narcotics and precursor chemicals. While the Arellano Félix brothers in Tijuana and the Juárez cartel cast their lot with the Gulf cartel, it encountered ferocious opposition from the Sinaloans and their allies in the Milenio, Jalisco and Colima organizations. The number of drug-related murders in Michoacán climbed from a few dozen in 2000 to 543 in 2006, before falling to 295 in 2007—with 216 deaths reported during the first eleven and a half months of 2008, including victims of the September 15 "Morelia massacre." As leader of the PAN's deputies from 2000 to 2003, Calderón had a front-row seat from which to observe his predecessor's faux pas.

3

Calderón's Top Priority

IN SEEKING THE PRESIDENCY, Calderón—a moderate who hoisted the banner of the PAN—emphasized three major goals: creating jobs, combating poverty and fighting crime. By the time he took office, his first priority was to curb the activities of increasingly savage cartels that were involved in the production, distribution and export of drugs. During the five months between his July 2, 2006, victory and his swearing in, narcoviolence had taken the lives of more than 1,000 people, lofting the yearly total to 2,231, an increase from 1,537 in 2005 and 1,304 in 2004. In 2007, the drug-related death toll ascended to 2,794, soaring above 5,000 for 2008.

These murders often bore the mark of mafia-style executions.

For instance, on September 6, 2006, gunmen crashed into the seedy Sol y Sombra nightclub in Uruapan, Michoacán, fired shots into the air, ordered revelers to lie down, ripped open a plastic bag and lobbed five human heads onto the black-and-white dance floor. The desperados left behind a note hailing their act as "divine justice," carried out on behalf of La Familia, once a partner of the Gulf cartel. The day before the macabre pyrotechnics, the killers had seized their victims and hacked off their heads with bowie knives while the men writhed in pain. "You don't do something like that unless you want to send a big message," said a U.S. law enforcement official, speaking on condition of anonymity.

Mexican President Felipe Calderón walks past army officers during a ceremony to mark the Day of the Army at a military base in Tula, Mexico, Feb. 19, 2007. During the event, Calderón announced a 46 percent salary increase for the soldiers, who are becoming increasingly involved in the country's war against drug traffickers. A year later, he unveiled another pay boost, which averaged 500 pesos ($45) per month. (AP Photo/Gregory Bull)

Not only have these highly publicized cruelties engendered "a psychosis of fear" within the population, but they have also conveyed the idea that wrongdoers can act with impunity. Indeed, the government has lost control over portions of its country in a crisis of governability similar to Afghanistan. Violence has also become a nightmare in Tijuana, located to the south of San Diego, and even the famous tourist resort of Acapulco—once lauded as the Pearl of the Pacific—has been informally renamed "Narcopulco," since numerous murders have occurred in the area.

The rising influx of illegal substances, accompanied by mounting deaths and kidnappings, prompted U.S. Ambassador to Mexico Antonio O. Garza to warn Americans "to exercise all due caution," adding that "drug cartel members have been known to follow and harass U.S. citizens traveling in their vehicles, particularly in border areas including Nuevo Laredo and Matamoros in Tamaulipas state."

In mid-November 2007, the Bush Administration announced that it had requested $550 million as part of a $1.4 billion three-year allocation for the Mérida Initiative, with $500 million earmarked for the equipment and training of Mexican security agencies and $50 million for their counterparts in Central America. The U.S. Congress ultimately agreed on $400 million—with $333 million released in December 2008.

While concerned about trade in proscribed goods and its associated bloodshed, Calderón, the father of three young children, has also expressed alarm at the escalating internal consumption of substances once allocated for export. "I know the anguish and pain of mothers who realize, sometimes too late, that their children have fallen into the claws of drugs," he said. Mexico City authorities have identified some 4,000 locations in the capital where drugs are sold, often to preteens and teenagers. In early August 2007, Attorney General Medina Mora reported that drug addiction within the country had increased from 15 to 30 percent annually since 2000.

Equally upsetting is the allure a gangster's lifestyle has for youngsters in Michoacán's Tierra Caliente. Brenda, a 12-year-old carrying a .9mm toy pistol, told a researcher: "Here the narcos enjoy respect because they help the people and have a great deal of power. Not even mayors help as much when someone dies or doesn't have a job." In contrast, children who witness the savagery may either become traumatized or inured to the bloodshed as an expected, even acceptable, part of life.

CAGLECARTOONS.COM/TAB, THE CALGARY SUN

In the past, TV, radio and newspaper stories about the brazenness of cartels and their leaders pressured law-enforcement agencies to pursue the culprits. However, fear of the assassination of journalists and bombings of printing plants has prompted the *El Mañana* newspaper chain, which publishes editions in the border cities of Reynosa, Matamoros, Nuevo Laredo and others, to tone down or eliminate coverage of narco-crimes. A drug gang reportedly has added at least one American journalist to its hit list. The Paris-based Reporters without Frontiers cited 95 attacks on journalists during the first half of 2008, while a *World Journalists' Report on Press Freedom* castigated Mexico as "one of the most dangerous countries" for reporters in the world—with approximately 40 journalists killed, eight missing and scores threatened, intimidated or harassed during the last eight years.

In March 2008, the Mexican Senate approved a constitutional amendment that replaces closed-door proceedings with U.S.-style open trials, allows recorded phone calls to be introduced as evidence if one of the participants agrees and enables prosecutors to hold organized crime suspects without charge for up to 80 days. The overall issue is "one-half law and one-half existing structures and culture. The elimination of corruption and bureaucracy is not easy, even with legal tools," as stated by one jurist.

Announced on December 13, 2006, another proposal sought to incorporate 7,500 soldiers and 2,500 marines into the Federal Preventive Police (PFP) for three months, but floundered due to opposition from military personnel, who claimed that such a move would harm their salaries, benefits, opportunities for promotion and reputations. (As a result, only 600 soldiers and 50 marines have been assigned to the federal police agency.)

Criminal organizations have penetrated and corrupted the two federal police forces, the Federal Investigation Agency (AFI) and the PFP. Calderón is searching for a silver bullet in the form of a single force to replace the roughly 3,800 local, state and federal law-enforcement agencies. In theory, this amalgamated body would recruit assiduously vetted men and women, who would be meticulously trained in modern techniques, infused with respect for human rights, garbed in spiffy uniforms, awarded decent pay and benefits and provided credits to acquire a decent, affordable home. To begin with, Calderón is determined to merge the PFP, formally under the Ministry of Public Security (SSP), and the AFI, a dependency of the Attorney General's Office, which touts itself as the local version of the FBI. On October 21, 2008, the chief executive asked Congress to create under the SSP a single "Federal Police," which would eliminate the PFP and assume the investigative functions of the AFI, which would cease to exist.

The president has boosted by 30 percent funds in his proposed budget to fight rampant street crime and accelerate the pursuit of the sadistic, well-heeled narco-barons who operate major cartels. Nevertheless, he and Secretary of Public Security Genaro García Luna face implacable opposition to creating a cohesive national police unit from governors, some Security Cabinet members and key lawmakers and military chiefs who doubt the competency of a new force, which, they fear, would snatch resources away from the army and navy. Critics gained more ammunition in late September 2008, when the government had to mobilize 300 members of the PFP to oust some 100 AFI officers who had occupied their agency's headquarters to protest the consolidation of the two forces.

As important as money may be, the resources contemplated for 2009 are insufficient to hire enough investigators to conduct background checks, psychologists to assess personality traits, polygraph operators to ferret out liars, drug-testing specialists to identify addicts, human-rights experts to inculcate respect for civil liberties and law-enforcement professionals to examine thoroughly and train a cadre of tens of thousands of well-paid new recruits.

Suppose that lightning struck or the Virgin of Guadalupe reappeared to create a lean-clean-crime-busting machine. How long would the new gendarmes remain pure? Would displaced cops forgo minor shakedowns to engage in venal acts of gangsterism? The suggestion that the government will keep tabs on expelled bad actors lies in the realm of fantasy. In all fairness, a home of their own could provide good cops with a stake in the community as well as a means for superiors to observe unexpected lifestyle changes that could signal illicit behavior. Meanwhile, Calderón has established a Corps of Support Forces under his control. This detachment has neither special quarters nor distinctive uniforms. Instead, several dozen or several hundred of its members may be mobilized to embark upon specific assignments.

In mid-2007, concerns over rampant corruption prompted García Luna to relieve 284 high officials in the PFP and AFI of their positions. He pledged that each would be subjected to psychological analysis, drug tests, polygraph examinations, background probes and physical checkups.

The sordid reputation of law-enforcement personnel poses a major obstacle to attracting applications from middle-class young men and women. "They look upon policemen not as professionals but as strange creatures, as Martians," lamented García Luna.

Reasons for the trepidation were obvious on May 9, 2008, when Edgar Millán Gómez, 42, a high-ranking PFP officer who coordinated regional strikes against criminal organizations with other federal forces, perished in an ambush at his home in Mexico City. The killing came a week after Millán announced the arrest of 12 alleged hit men from the Sinaloa cartel.

The disdain for the police and their vulnerability has spurred the president to enlist citizens in his version of a neighborhood watch program called "Clean up Mexico." However the wave of narco-violence will limit the denunciation of criminal activities. Although devoted to family and close friends, most Mexicans evince a low sense of obligation to their community. Even worse, they fear that the police may be in league with the criminals. Army brass, who enjoy a much better reputation, hope to have more success with their dissemination of a telephone number and e-mail address through which anonymous tips can be sent.

Reliance on the Armed Forces

The obstacles to creating reliable civilian agencies force the chief executive to depend on Mexico's armed forces, which—while not free from corruption—are less contaminated than the several thousand federal, state, local and quasi-private police forces. Calderón began by mending relations between the presidency and the army after his predecessor, Vicente Fox, raised hackles among the brass. Fox had named a mediocre "desk general," Clemente Vega García, as defense secretary; had appointed a lower-ranking general as attorney general, a position superior to defense secretary; and had created a National Security Cabinet led by a left-wing politician, who failed to garner respect from more-experienced officials supposedly under his purview.

To make matters worse, Fox slighted the military in a post-9/11 interview on *Larry King Live.* When the TV host asked if his nation would join the war against terrorism, the inept Mexican leader stated, "Militarily speaking, we don't count. I mean, we are not a military country. We don't have a strong army. That is not the way we contribute." This comment ricocheted through the National Defense Ministry like a photon in a laser cavity.

In contrast, Calderón has wasted no time in courting the armed forces. Initially, he had feared a disruption of his inaugural ceremonies by loyalists of Andrés Manuel López Obrador, the PRD's messianic presidential nominee, who subsequently proclaimed himself the nation's "legitimate president" and continues to barnstorm the country. To guard against this threat, the chief executive-elect received from Fox the presidential sash carried by a cadet from the Heroic Military College, Mexico's version of West Point, just after midnight on December 1, 2006.

After the military had ensured that the public investiture before Congress took place with minimal disruptions, later in the morning, Calderón went to the Campo Marte near Los Pinos (Mexico's presidential residence and offices). Accompanied by Defense Secretary Guillermo Galván Galván and Navy Secretary Mariano Francisco Saynez Mendoza, he reviewed troops, received a 21-gun salute and raised an enormous flag before praising the loyal men and women in uniform whose "commitment to the security and well-being of Mexicans must be justly recognized and compensated."

During his first address to the nation, he stressed austerity but promised to enlarge the budget of the armed forces and other security institutions. In February 2007, he awarded a pay raise as high as 46 percent to soldiers, while cutting 10 percent from his own salary. A year later, he announced another increase. One of the goals of boosting compensation is to reduce the contagion of desertions, which numbered 150,000 personnel, including at least 1,560 special forces between 2000 and 2009, and totaled 18,128 in 2008. Defectors have provided well-trained recruits for the cartels.

Calderón even visited the 43rd military zone in Apatzingán, a no-man's-land of narco-activities in Michoacán. There he donned a floppy military tunic and sported an olive-green field hat bearing five stars and the national shield—all symbols of the commander in chief—to underscore his solidarity with the federal forces assigned to confront drug traffickers. On another occasion, the president's two young sons wore military uniforms as they observed the 2007 Independence Day parade

Mexican soldiers stand over a detained man after a gun battle that left four
dead traffickers in the city of Apatzingán, Mexico, May 7, 2007. Mexican
drug cartels armed with powerful weapons and angered by a nationwide military crackdown are striking back, killing soldiers in bold, daily attacks.
(AP Photo/Agencia Esquema)

alongside their parents and the secretaries of defense and navy.
Meanwhile, the government commended the armed forces
in television commercials, while appointing to attaché posts
in distant countries generals threatened by cartels. Calderón's
deference toward the military and his increased use of military personnel to combat rampant drug violence quickly im-
proved his approval rating. The armed forces have committed
themselves to confronting the cartels because of their respect
for the president, their nationalistic creed and their concern
about the loss of sovereignty over broad areas to which the
narco-barons have laid siege. In addition, military personnel
enjoy greater protection than civilians who, even if they have
several domiciles, find themselves at risk. Still, critics question

the legality of the military's performance of police functions.

A New Approach

To set the tone for his regime, Calderón wasted no time before extraditing drug kingpins to the United States. Although Fox had been eager to act, the Mexican Supreme Court had tied his hands on the grounds that Mexican citizens could not be tried in countries that imposed sanctions not authorized at home—namely, sentences longer than 60 years and capital punishment. Moreover, Fox had also encountered abstruse injunctions known as *amparos,* multilayered lower courts, and Kafkaesque procedural technicalities. Nonetheless, he managed to send scores of fugitives to the United States, many of whom were citizens of America or third countries.

During Fox's term, the number of those extradited rose from 17 in 2001 to 63 in 2006. However, with the exception of the May 2001 extradition of the right-hand man of the notorious Arellano Félix Organization (known as the AFO or the Tijuana cartel), few high-level chiefs are included in this number. In November 2005, the Supreme Court partially reversed its earlier ruling and therefore permitted the extradition of Francisco Rafael Arellano Félix, who at that time was the highest-level trafficker sent to the United States under Fox.

Calderón's appointment of José Luis Santiago Vasconcelos, an expert in extraditions, as assistant attorney general for judicial and international affairs, foreshadowed his readiness to banish bad actors. Seven weeks after taking office, the new administration handed over 15 suspects to U.S. authorities. The most infamous of the group was Cárdenas Guillén, who since his 2003 arrest had run the Gulf cartel from his well-appointed cell at La Palma, a maximum-security prison 35 miles west of Mexico City.

Three other extradited potentates appeared on the Bush Administration's "kingpin list," which included Héctor "El Güero"

Palma Salazar, a top lieutenant of El Chapo Guzmán, leader of the mighty Sinaloa cartel and the sworn enemy of the Gulf cartel.

"El Güero" Palma epitomizes the swaggering drug lord. He paid incredible amounts in protection fees to the Guadalajara police, carried a handgun encrusted with diamonds and emeralds and dressed in a flamboyant style embellished by gold chains and snakeskin boots. When arrested in 1995 after his Lear jet crashed in Nayarit, he was accompanied by seven gunmen and 33 heavily armed members of the Federal Judicial Police, who served as his bodyguards. The composition of his team confirmed what most Mexicans had long known: "The police are for sale, and the criminals are buying.…" In addition, authorities extradited two other arch criminals in the Arellano Félix Organization centered in Tijuana. All told, Calderón extradited 166 men and women to the U.S., Europe and Latin America during his first two years in office.

In July 2007, Santiago Vasconcelos asked Washington to extradite to Mexico Zhenli Ye Gon, an affluent Chinese-Mexican businessman. Earlier in the year, U.S. law-enforcement agencies had discovered that Ye Gon possessed a trove of cash in his opulent Mexico City mansion. The Americans passed along the information to the PGR, which accordingly searched the premises and found $227 million in cash and traveler's checks. In addition, the PGR found a cache of luxury automobiles, high-powered rifles and equipment to make amphetamine pills.

This wealth undoubtedly came from the importation of pseudoephedrine, a decongestant used to manufacture methamphetamine, a synthetic stimulant known as "meth" or "ice." His import volume exceeded two to three times the country's legitimate needs. Despite a pending arrest warrant, Ye Gon took possession of at least four more large shipments of chemicals through the Pacific port of Lázaro Cárdenas, Michoacán, marketed it to cartels and independent laboratories, obtained government-issued identification papers and traveled back and forth to the United States at will. On July 23, 2007, DEA agents captured Ye Gon in Wheaton, Maryland. Mexican officials have requested his extradition, but it appears likely that U.S. authorities will try him in a U.S. court on drug-trafficking and money-laundering charges first.

In contrast with Fox, Calderón has sent large contingents of federal police and troops to combat the insidious lawbreakers. His first dozen or more deployments averaged around 2,000 individuals. He has also dispatched units to more areas of the country while not notifying the mayor (Tijuana) or governors (Michoacán, Guerrero, etc.) in advance of strikes. Fox continuously altered his priorities in what appeared as a "flavor-of-the-month" style of governing. In the face of a mounting body count, in 2005 he unveiled his "Safe Mexico Plan" ("Plan México Se-

Santiago Vasconcelos, deputy attorney general of Mexico, left, listens as account manager David Martin describes some of his company's video security devices at a conference on global border security, May 21, 2008, in Austin, Texas. Vasconcelos, who, delivered the keynote speech at the conference, died in a plane crash on November 4, 2008. (AP Photo/Harry Cabluck)

guro") with the dispatch of forces to Nuevo León, Tijuana and Acapulco. But Fox's defense secretary did not want to involve the army in interrogations or assign it to guarding checkpoints and conducting searches. He feared that "drug work would inevitably discredit the armed forces, as soldiers became abusive after months of being stationed in impoverished areas under high degrees of stress and boredom."

Instead, the military concentrated on interdiction, crop eradication and intelligence gathering. Fox may have shied away from a scorched-earth policy in the run-up to the bitter 2006 presidential contest. In contrast, Calderón has lasered in on the crime issue, accentuating his de-

U.S. Counternarcotics Assistance to Mexico*

FISCAL YEAR	(MILLIONS OF DOLLARS)
1999	8.0
2000	4.1
2001	10.0
2002	12.0
2003	12.0
2004	37.0
2005	39.7
2006	39.6
2007	36.7
2008 (Estimated)	26.6
2008 (Supplemental Estimate)	215.5
2009 (Supplemental Estimate)	48.0
2009 (Requested)	477.82

*Allocations made by the Bureau of International Narcotics Control and Law Enforcement account of the U.S. Department of State.

SOURCE: U.S. DEPARTMENT OF STATE, BUREAU OF INTERNATIONAL NARCOTICS CONTROL AND LAW ENFORCEMENT, VARIOUS REPORTS WWW.STATE.GOV/P/INL/RLS/NRCRPT; AND MARK P. SULLIVAN ET AL., CONGRESSIONAL RESEARCH SERVICE, REPORT TO CONGRESS, MEXICO-U.S. RELATIONS: ISSUES FOR CONGRESS, NOVEMBER 14, 2008 WWW.FAS.ORG/SGP/CRS/ROW/RL327244.

termination to "take back the country from criminals."

President Calderón's administration has publicly criticized the U.S. government for supplying inadequate assistance to Mexico. The U.S. State Department reported that in fiscal year 2006, Mexico received almost $40 million for its antidrug ventures, compared with the $600 million allocated to Colombia. The White House provided an estimated $36.7 million in 2007—with the initial estimate for 2008 falling to $26.6 million on the grounds that Mexico boasts the world's 13th-largest economy. This figure has shot up with the disbursements of Mérida Initiative monies.

In mid-June 2007, Attorney General Eduardo Medina Mora, a key architect of Mexico's anticrime strategy, deplored Washington's policy as "cynical with respect to consumption." A conservative, a product of the private sector and a former executive in his nation's intelligence service (Center for Intelligence and National Security—CISEN), Medina Mora said that the United States was "cynical" because it only saw the problem outside its borders and did little to reduce the domestic demand for illegal drugs. He also excoriated as "absurd" the lax gun-control laws north of the Rio Grande, where border towns are home to some 1,200 gun vendors who sell everything from fragmentation grenades to rocket launchers. The UN, he stressed, estimates that 70 percent of the revenue generated by drug transactions remains in the places where the substances are consumed.

Calderón has put together a more cohesive team than Fox's "Montessori Cabinet," a puckish allusion to its members' preference for self-expression rather than teamwork. The attorney general shares responsibility for the antidrug effort with Public Security Secretary García Luna, Defense Secretary Galván, Navy Secretary Saynez and Government Secretary Fernando Gómez Mont, who replaced Juan Camilo Mouriño Terrazo, a member of Calderón's inner circle who died in a plane crash on November 4, 2008. Guillermo Valdés Castellanos, another Calderón confidant, heads CISEN, which falls under the compass of the government ministry. Sigrid Arzt Colunga, an expert in security matters, works as technical secretary to the National Security Council, composed of the president, the director of CISEN and nine secretaries, whose ministries are involved in the war against organized crime. Finance ministry officials concentrate on drug-laundering schemes. Until his forced resignation in early September 2008, Roberto Campa Cifrián functioned as executive secretary of the larger National Public Security Council, which acts as a liaison between the federal government and state and local officials.

State and local governments remain a cesspool of corruption. There are several "agreements" between kingpins and mayors and governors. Many gangs prefer to cut deals with mayors to save money. However, when a mayor and his governor attempt to safeguard different criminal organizations, the ensuing war is usually won by the governor's favorite.

The tables are now being reversed. It is an open secret that some state and local authorities must now pay protection fees to Los Zetas or their partners—with the amount ranging from $2,000 to $30,000 a month. His refusal to fork over extortion money may explain the murder, in early October 2008, of Salvador Vergara, mayor of Ixtapan de la Sal, a tourist town in Mexico State.

Although Calderón's entourage shows more harmony than Fox's, intramural clashes have occurred. The sensational revelation of Ye Gon's fortune excited jurisdictional tensions between the Attorney General's Office and the Public Security Ministry. Rumors abound that the officer who developed a thick archive on Ye Gon took advantage of this information to blackmail the Chinese-Mexican's contacts. Reportedly, José Nemesio Lugo Félix, head of an intelligence unit that focused on cartels, threatened to blow the whistle on his unscrupulous underling before an unidentified gunman killed him on May 15, 2007. García Luna has also crossed swords with Santiago Vasconcelos, who left his post in the Attorney General's Office two months before perishing in the airplane disaster that took Mouriño Terrazo's life.

As deputy attorney general in 2005, Santiago Vasconcelos claimed that corruption suffused the ranks of AFI, then headed by García Luna. García Luna, whom the key military officers dislike because of his identification with the Fox regime, repeatedly clashed with Campa Cifrián before the latter stepped down as well. To bring discipline to his fractious entourage, in October 2008 Calderón named Jorge E. Tello Peón, a distinguished, veteran law-enforcement expert, as a virtual czar for national security. Marisela Morales Ibañez, who in September 2008 was appointed deputy attorney general for the specialized investigation of organized crime, has earned praise for attacking the cartels. Her predecessor was charged with leaking information to drug lords.

Morales Ibañez played a key role in raiding a sprawling mansion, which contained a zoo with exotic animals, in a posh Mexico City neighborhood. Among those apprehended in this foray were 11 Colombians believed to form an important link in supplying cocaine to Mexican drug lords. In October 2008 authorities also arrested Jesús Reynaldo "El Rey" Zambada García, brother of Sinaloa cartel honcho Ismael "El Mayo" Zambada García, who was in a life-and-death struggle with the Beltrán Leyva crime family for dominion over drug flows through the crime-suffused Mexico City airport.

The assignment of the armed forces to undertake law-enforcement duties has excited charges of human rights abuses. On June 1, 2007, soldiers at a checkpoint in Sinaloa fired more than a dozen rounds into an automobile, killing three children and two unarmed women. In the aftermath of the bloodbath, the

53

defense ministry, which has established a human rights office, arrested three officers and 16 soldiers. Spokesmen for nongovernmental organizations (NGOs) fear that trying the accused in a military court will yield either exoneration or light punishments. While abuses continue, Galván has moved to punish individuals and members of units who violate human rights, such as those involved in the Sinaloa killings. In fact, military courts often deal out harsher sentences than their civilian counterparts.

The defense secretary has also given more authority to the dozen regional commanders who once had to clear even limited forays with Mexico City. In an open letter to a Tijuana daily, General Sergio Aponte Polito, commander of the Second Military Zone, claimed as well as named law-enforcement officials who had cast their lot with elements of the underworld. Professor Roderic Ai Camp, the leading U.S. expert on the Mexican armed forces, called the communiqué "extraordinary" because it "illustrates beautifully the greater independence such commanders are playing." However, superiors moved the outspoken Aponte, who had raised hackles among politicians, to the post of president of the Supreme Military Tribunal.

Criticism aside, in a late May 2008 poll, 81 percent of respondents applauded the president's military strategy against drug-traffickers, even though 56 percent of those interviewed believed the cartels were winning the battle. *Proceso* newsmagazine scorned the antidrug initiative as "Calderón's Iraq" and a "lost war." Former Foreign Minister Jorge Castañeda has castigated the president for failing to clarify his objectives. "Do we want to defeat and banish the cartels, or just force them back into their lairs? Do we want to spare Mexico (but not the United States) by sealing off Mexico's southern border, thereby rerouting drug shipments from South America to the United States via detours in the Caribbean and the gulf?" he queried. Police venality has left the president with two alternatives: either sit on his hands or deploy military units.

If he is to achieve long-term success against criminal organizations, President Calderón will have to reform the nation's rapacious police forces, the ineffective and cumbersome judicial system and the inadequate and poorly run prison system.

Prospects for U.S.–Mexican Narcotics Relations?

Can Calderón take back his country from the drug cartels and reduce the flow of narcotics into the United States? There are three approaches to dealing with the criminal syndicates that he could pursue in tandem with the United States.

•Continue the War on Drugs?

The likelihood of success is remote in view of the astronomical fortunes derived from the production, shipment and distribution of illegal substances. Narco-dollars contaminate everyone they touch, including U.S. federal officials and local law-enforcement officers. Corruption so engulfs Mexico's legal system that the professional, honest, national police force advocated by Calderón appears to be a pipe dream. At best, the Mexican government, with help from Washington, can try to limit the scope of the narco-industry. Continued reliance on the military to pursue drug lords is a recipe to amplify corruption and human-rights abuses within the armed forces, an institution that has traditionally enjoyed a high level of public esteem.

Even as the current drive against organized crime leads to the arrest of mostly third- and fourth-tier gangsters, the top dogs will be increasingly difficult to capture because of the decentralization under way within the main organizations. With the resources at their disposal, the cell-like cartels will have little difficulty protecting themselves from the police thanks to their recruitment of army deserters and veterans. To keep its elite GAFE (special forces) from joining the cartels, as scores have already done, the army raised the salary for soldiers to $1,100 per month in 2007. To spite this effort, the cartels promptly doubled that amount as the standard pay for its own "troops." "The [Mexican] army can no more control this situation than the Americans and the British can control the situation in Iraq," insisted security analyst Samuel González. He explains that "the army can make its presence felt and perhaps limit some of the most extreme expressions of the violence, but the structural causes remain." Recent reports reveal that cartels are increasingly relying on the thousands of so-called gatekeepers, individuals who have day-to-day control over plazas, guaranteeing that appropriate fees are collected and sent to cartel coffers. They ensure that appropriate payments are made to police and military personnel to foster smooth operations. Some experts estimate that they may be facilitating the transport of up to 80 percent of the drugs across the border into the United States.

Even as the government uses force against narco-traffickers, it must improve its intelligence capability and "follow the money," as the U.S. Customs Service did so skillfully in Operation Casablanca. In Mexico, a customer paying cash can purchase anything from airplanes, to helicopters, to armored vehicles, to hotel rooms, without presenting a passport, voting credential, or any other credible document. The nations' banks, ever wary of losing clients, must be persuaded to report large deposits to the government. Even more of an Achilles' heel is Mexico's customs service, which is a sewer of venality, corruption, disorganization and cronyism.

If, by chance, "Lady Luck" smiled on Calderón and he successfully thwarted drug activities, an international cucaracha effect would take place—with Asian, Middle Eastern and Russian suppliers replacing Mexican distributors. In the interim, Mexican mobsters would have to allocate more attention to the local market as they undertake kidnappings, murders-for-hire and bank robberies, as has occurred in Tijuana.

Nevertheless, the Bush Administration and its Mexican counterpart successfully lobbied the U.S. Congress to approve the Mérida Initiative. By late December 2008, the U.S. Department of State had disbursed $333 million of the funds earmarked for Mexico in the FY2008 supplemental spending budget; Congress will release another $43 million when internal reporting requirements are met, and $24 million to administer the plan. In all likelihood, the legislators would have turned down the proposal if they had voted after the August 1 discovery of the decomposed body of 14-year-old Fernando Martí. At least one Mexican federal police official was implicated in the kidnapping of the youngster, the son of a wealthy businessman who catalyzed a massive anticrime demonstration in Mexico City. The assistance will be used for nonintrusive inspection equipment such as ion scanners, gamma-ray scanners, X-ray vans and canine units for Mexico and Central America; improved and secure telecommunications systems that collect criminal information in Mexico; technical training to strengthen the judicial system; software to track cases and investigations through the system; witness protection programs; eight used Bell 412 EP helicopters and two Cessna 208 Caravan surveillance aircraft; and equipment, training and community action programs in Central American countries to implement antigang measures. Washington is also eager to shore up Calderón's "Platform Mexico," conceived to develop a modern and efficient data system that will facilitate the exchange of information about criminal activities between and among the nation's states.

To win approval of the controversial legislation, Mexican and U.S. officials trumpeted Mexico's recent success against traffickers such as the record 23-ton cocaine bust in the Pacific port of Manzanillo in late 2007. In commenting on the biggest seizure of this drug in the country's history, U.S. Ambassador Garza called the coup "further proof of President Calderón's commitment to cripple drug lords and bring them to justice."

Authorities also arrested Sandra Ávila Beltrán, 45, who supposedly managed public relations and helped ship cocaine from Colombia to Mexico for the Sinaloa cartel. The redoubtable "Queen of the Pacific" is a niece of Félix Gallardo, yet she described herself as a simple housewife who derived her income from renting homes and selling clothes.

To show its readiness to cooperate, the Bureau of Alcohol, Tobacco, Firearms and Explosives (ATF), an agency of the U.S. Department of Justice, unveiled Project Gunrunner. Under this program, the ATF plans to deploy resources strategically on the southwest border to deny weapons to criminal organizations and to combat firearms-related violence along the frontier.

Mexico's Attorney General's Office has even raised the possibility of relocating the country from center stage to the wings of narco-trafficking, provided that three things transpire: (1) Operación Limpieza (Operation Cleanup), designed to prevent small cocaine-ferrying aircraft from Colombia, Panama and Venezuela, succeeds in forcing South American producers to circumvent Mexico as they concentrate more on the growing European market; (2) the United States, which now produces 70 percent of the marijuana it consumes, manages to meet its own demand by growing 100 percent; and (3) suppliers of precursor chemicals in Asia and Germany realize that they can earn vastly higher profits by manufacturing methamphetamines at home—rather than in Mexican laboratories—for direct export to America.

Calderón realizes that he must complement law-and-order policies with a socioeconomic plan that will smash monopolies and other bottlenecks that impede sustained growth and international competition, overhaul the antiquated health-care system, revitalize his nation's infrastructure, improve public schools that have been colonized by the venal Education Workers Union and regain control of convict-run prisons where killings and mutinies abound. There is also the imperative to boost tax collections, which as a percentage of gross domestic product fall below 12 percent, on a par with Haiti, an economic basket case.

•Focus on Demand Side: Education and Treatment?

It seems hypocritical of Washington to blame Mexico for the influx of drugs when Americans generate most of the demand. Only when U.S. officials accept co-responsibility with Mexico by placing as much weight on curtailing consumption as they do on reducing supply will progress take place. Drugs have become an international challenge, and as Professor Bruce M. Bagley, an expert on drug trafficking at the University of Miami, has observed, "the Mexican-U.S. trade is a manifestation—virulent to be sure—of that global trade."

Escalating demand requires much greater attention to prevention, education and treatment, especially in prisons, where small-time drug dealers go behind bars as amateurs only to emerge years later as hardened professionals. The dubious record of America's vaunted War on Drugs argues strongly for the decriminalization of the possession and sale of small quantities of controlled substances.

•Thinking about the Unthinkable: Decriminalization?

In off-the-record conversations, scores of well-known politicians from across the spectrum endorse decriminalizing, if not legalizing, the possession of marijuana for personal use by adults. Many also believe in treating addiction to cocaine and heroin as a health concern rather than criminal behavior and thus permitting addicts to obtain controlled substances with doctors' prescriptions. Mike Gravel, a former U.S. senator from Alaska and a maverick outside contender for the 2008 Democratic presidential nomination, publicly expressed these views, not because he favors drug use, but due to the failure of the nation's supply-side approach.

Some elected officials have gone even further. In 1999, New Mexico's governor became the highest-ranking elected official to advocate the legalization of drugs. Governor Gary Johnson rationalized that everything from marijuana to heroin ought to be legalized because the U.S. antidrug effort is "an expensive bust." "Control it, regulate it, tax it," Johnson elaborated on the use of recreational drugs, because, he asserts, "if you legalize it, we might actually have a healthier society." Johnson, a Republican, said the nation's war on drugs has been a multibillion-dollar failure that has thrown too many people in prison. He queries, "should you go to jail for just doing drugs?" Johnson states, "I say no. I say you shouldn't." By at least one estimate, the United States spends $40 billion a year trying to intercept shipments and arrest drug dealers and users.

But in spite of all the federal and local law enforcement attempts, a mere 5 to 15 percent of the illegal drugs entering the United States is actually seized. The rest of the drugs feed a $200-billion-a-year illegal business that caters to an estimated 13 million Americans each month. The Rand Corporation has found that treatment is far more cost-effective than interdiction in reducing the use of cocaine. At the very least, the United States should legalize the medicinal use of narcotics so that doctors can prescribe doses to patients who will benefit from ingredients found in them.

In 2006, the Fox administration introduced a bill to decriminalize the possession of small amounts of the most popular illegal drugs. Under his initiative, penalties would be relaxed for possessing 0.5 grams of cocaine, five grams of marijuana and 25 milligrams of heroin, among other substances. "Mexico is trying to make the right choices." The Mexican legislation will "go a long way toward reducing opportunities for police corruption and harassment in their interactions with ordinary citizens," stated Ethan Nadelmann, executive director of the Drug Policy Alliance, a group that favors ending the War on Drugs. In contrast, Washington came out strongly against the measure, which the Mexican president ultimately shelved; the bloodshed related to obtaining and holding plazas continues unabated. Calderón has revived a similar initiative.

The greater portion of Washington's international antinarcotics spending goes to Latin America and the Caribbean. Despite militarization and robust funding for the drug war, illegal substances continue to flood into the United States. In fact, the crackdown in Mexico has had little effect on cocaine consumption in the United States even as the price of the drug has fluctuated between $96 and $119 per ounce and its purity has declined by 11 percent.

Conclusion

Optimists hope that the Morelia calamity will help Calderón throw the cartels on the defensive, gain cooperation from a frightened public and facilitate the arrest of drug kingpins.

Unless this rosy picture emerges, Mexico and the United States will have their hands full just managing the narco-trafficking and attendant violence. For their part, the criminal syndicates are reconfiguring their organizations, upgrading recruitment campaigns, developing their own militias, levying taxes on businesses in their domains, buying expensive properties, acquiring athletic teams, organizing underground financial institutions, selling protection to municipal governments, providing jobs in distressed regions, forging relations with their counterparts in other countries, contributing to religious projects, exacting "tolls" to cross plazas they control and paying musicians to compose ballads that extol the virtues of their leaders. In an apparent ploy to soften its image for brutality, the Gulf cartel has even offered a $5 million reward for information leading to the capture of the Independence Day grenade throwers who allegedly belong to La Familia. Does this offer connote fear and disintegration or does it signify that Mexico is moving toward dual sovereignty between the elected government, on the one hand, and the drug barons on the other?

Talking It Over

A Note for Students and Discussion Groups

This issue of the HEADLINE SERIES, like its predecessors, is published for every serious reader, specialized or not, who takes an interest in the subject. Many of our readers will be in classrooms, seminars, or community discussion groups. Particularly with them in mind, we present below some discussion questions—suggested as a starting point only—and references for further reading, as well as pertinent online resources.

Discussion Questions

While the last two Mexican leaders have both attempted to tackle the expanding power and influence of drug cartels, how has Calderón's approach differed from that of his predecessor, Vicente Fox?

While Calderón has sent over 30,000 military troops to directly fight the drug cartels, the number of drug-related deaths for 2008 exceeded 5,000, far surpassing the totals of the last two years. How would you evaluate the accomplishments of Calderón's policies so far? How have the activities of the cartels evolved to counter Calderón's aggressive approach?

Why did Calderón choose to use the military as opposed to the police as his main instrument in Mexico's current War on Drugs?

Aside from a security- and military-based approach toward the drug cartels operating in Mexico, are there alternative methods that could be employed to combat their influence and power? What factors have created the conditions that foster groups like Los Zetas or "narco juniors"?

Experts have noted that in order to fight an effective antidrug war, reform of Mexico's police and judiciary system will also be necessary. What has Calderón done or attempted to do on these fronts?

What role do you see the United States playing in Calderón's offensive against the drug cartels in Mexico? Does the proposed Mérida Initiative do too little or too much to assist Mexico in its antidrug efforts? Moreover, do you think Calderón's efforts can succeed when demand for drugs in the United States continues to remain steady and drug trafficking is a vastly lucrative enterprise?

Recently, Mexican Finance Minister Agustín Carstens stated that "crime and violence" has "cost Mexico one percentage point of GDP growth each year, the result of lost sales, jobs and investment. Crime increases business costs by 5–10 percent a year." Meanwhile, the government has allocated increasing funds to the military for security-related expenditures. With a global economic slowdown and falling oil prices, will Calderón be able to afford his campaign against the cartels?

As the author notes, "Jorge Castañeda has castigated the president for failing to clarify his objectives. 'Do we want to defeat and banish the cartels, or just force them back into their lairs? Do we want to spare Mexico (but not the United States) by sealing off Mexico's southern border, thereby rerouting drug shipments from South America to the United States via detours in the Caribbean and the gulf?'" What do you think Calderón's long-term goal is, and how would you define "success" in Mexico's current drug war?

Annotated Reading List

Cook, Colleen W., "Mexico's Drug Cartels." Congressional Research Service Report for Congress RL34215, October 16, 2007. www.fas.org/sgp/crs/row/RL34215.pdf. An overview of Mexican cartels and their operations, including the spread of Mexican drug production and cartel cells to the United States.

Ford, Jess T., "U.S. Assistance Has Helped Mexican Counternarcotics Efforts, but the Flow of Illicit Drugs into the United States Remains High." United States Government Accountability Office Testimony Before the Subcommittee on the Western Hemisphere, Committee on Foreign Affairs, October 27, 2007. www.gao.gov/new.items/d08215t.pdf. A detailed U.S. government report on U.S.–Mexico drug trafficking and relevant counternarcotics efforts, including policy recommendations.

Grayson, George W., "Los Zetas: The Ruthless Army Spawned by a Mexican Drug Cartel." Foreign Policy Research Institute E-Notes, May 2008. www.fpri.org/enotes/200805.grayson.loszetas.html. A closer look at Los Zetas, and why some experts argue that it has "become the biggest, most serious threat to [Mexico's] security."

Grillo, Ioan, "Mexico's Cocaine Capital." **Time,** August 14, 2008. Narco-violence in Sinaloa and Culiacán have residents wondering if the power of the drug cartels has surpassed that of the government.

Logan, Sam, and Kairies, Kate, "U.S. Drug Habit Migrates to Mexico." Americas Policy Program Special Report. Center for International Policy, February 7, 2007. http://americas.irc-online.org/pdf/reports/0702meth.pdf. While drug manufacturing and trafficking headlines Mexico's war on drugs, the rise in Mexico's own domestic drug consumption requires another dimension in Calderón's drug policies.

Mares, David A., **Drug Wars and Coffeehouses: The Political Economy of the International Drug Trade.** Washington, DC, CQ Press, 2005. A comprehensive yet succinct breakdown of the international drug trade and the respective policies enacted to counter it, with extensive case studies and policy analysis.

Meyer, Maureen, et al., "At a Crossroads: Drug Trafficking, Violence and the Mexican State." Washington Office on Latin America and the Beckley Foundation Drug Policy Programme Briefing Paper 13 (November 2007). www.wola.org/media/Beckley%20Briefing13usletter.pdf. This brief examines how the U.S. government has shaped Mexico's counter-drug efforts and questions the long-term implications of using a militarized approach to combat drug activities.

Payan, Tony, **The Three U.S.-Mexico Border Wars: Drugs, Immigration, and Homeland Security.** Westport, CT, Praeger Security International, 2006. A detailed look at the history and evolution of these intertwined issues and how they have shaped current border policies.

Sarukhan, Arturo, "Real Solutions for Challenges on the Mexico-U.S. Border: The Mérida Initiative." Heritage Foundation Lecture #1095 (Delivered 28 April 2008). www.heritage.org/research/LatinAmerica/hl1095.cfm. Mexico's ambassador to the United States explains why the Mérida Initiative is a vital step in the counternarcotics efforts of Mexico and the United States.

Suau, Anthony, "Mexico's Drug Wars—A Photo Essay." **Time** online. www.time.com/time/photogallery/0,29307,1651420,00.html. A photo essay of the violent struggle between drug cartels and the federal government in northern Mexico.

Online Resources

Inter-American Dialogue, 1211 Connecticut Ave NW, Suite 510, Washington, DC 20036; (202) 822-9002; Fax (202) 822-9553. www.thedialogue.org. A leading center for policy analysis, exchange and communication on issues in Western Hemisphere affairs, with a specific program focusing on Mexico.

PBS Frontline: Drug Wars, www.pbs.org/wgbh/pages/frontline/shows/drugs. An in-depth, interactive look from both sides of the battlefield at the 30-year history of America's war on drugs, including an extensive overview of U.S.-Mexico drug issues, an exploration of Mexican cartel activities in the United States, interviews with DEA agents investigating Mexican drug cartels and links to other resources. **Political Database of the Americas,** Georgetown University, Box 571026, Washington, DC 20057; (202) 687-0146; Fax (202) 687-0141. http://pdba.georgetown.edu. The site provides resources on all aspects of government and policymaking in the countries of Latin America, with links to relevant newspapers, journals and international organizations, along with its own publications and working papers—with sections on transnational organized crime and citizen security.

Washington Office on Latin America, 1666 Connecticut Avenue NW, Suite 400, Washington, DC 20009; (202) 797-2171; Fax (202) 797-2172. www.wola.org. WOLA brings together government officials and NGOs in the promotion of human rights, democracy and socioeconomic justice throughout Latin America. The site provides news, publications and links to a variety of sources on Latin American policies and their impact.

White House Office of National Drug Control Policy, P.O. Box 6000, Rockville, MD 20849; (800) 666-3332; Fax (301) 519-5212. www.whitehousedrugpolicy.gov. The online home of the ONDCP, the main government body responsible for evaluating, coordinating and overseeing international and domestic antidrug efforts.

APPENDIX 1
Mexican Cartels

SINALOA CARTEL

Founders: Jaime Herrera Nevares; Ernesto "Don Neto" Fonseca Carrillo (captured April 8, 1985); Eduardo "El Lalo" Fernández; Jorge Favela Escobar; Pedro Áviles Pérez (killed September 9, 1978); Miguel Ángel Félix Gallardo (captured April 8, 1989); and Héctor Luis "El Güero" Palma (captured June 24, 1995), who was extradited to the United States to face drug-trafficking charges (January 19, 2007).

Current Leaders: Arturo Beltrán Leyva and his brothers have not only broken with Joaquín "El Chapo" Guzmán Loera and Ismael "El Mayo" Zambada García, but have declared war on their former allies. Another individual of significance, Juan José "El Azul" Esparagoza Moreno, is a murky figure who enjoys productive linkages with the Sinaloa cartel and other criminal bands because of his role as a "consiglieri," along with the respect he commands for his negotiating prowess.

Structure of Operation: The Sinaloa cartel was founded in the 1970s, and its power and wealth expanded a decade later, driven by the imperative for Colombians to ship cocaine through Mexico. The cartel's predominant areas of operation are in northwest Mexico, Sinaloa, Durango, Chihuahua, Baja California (Mexicali), Sonora (Nogales, Agua Prieta and San Luis Río Colorado), Tamaulipas (Nuevo Laredo), Nuevo León (Monterrey), Michoacán and Guerrero (Acapulco and other areas). The Sinaloa cartel moves cocaine, heroin and marijuana to American consumers. Guzmán Loera claims to shun unnecessary violence, yet he unleashes his tough "Sinaloan Cowboys" and police protectors against foes. That he continually vanishes when efforts are made to capture him has invested El Chapo with an almost mystic quality like that enjoyed

---

Due to the nature of this subject, the information, although current when the book went to press, is likely to change.

by revolutionary Francisco "Pancho" Villa in the first part of the twentieth century.

Background: Beginning in the late 1940s, Jaime Herrera Nevares, a former state judicial policeman, emerged as the patriarch of a potent criminal syndicate based in the mountaintop village of Los Herreras, Durango. The Herrera organization pioneered a farm-to-the-arm heroin structure that cultivated opium poppy, processed and packaged heroin and transported it to Chicago along what became known as the Heroin Highway. There it was either sold locally or distributed to other U.S. cities. This network proved extremely difficult to penetrate because family members controlled the entire heroin distribution scheme.

The Herrera family cooperated with Ernesto "Don Neto" Fonseca and Jorge Favela Escobar, who drew attention as key Sinaloan drug operatives in the 1950s and 1960s. After the government launched Operation Condor (1977) to eradicate drugs in the Golden Triangle, many bosses settled in the "sanctuary city" of Guadalajara. These included Fonseca Carrillo (arrested April 8, 1985), Pedro Áviles Pérez (killed September 9, 1978), Miguel Angel Félix Gallardo (arrested April 8, 1989), Rafael Caro Quintero (arrested April 4, 1985), Ismael "El Mayo" Zambada, Arturo Beltrán Leyva and his brothers, "El Chapo" Gúzman Loera and "El Azul" Esparragoza Moreno. During this period, they shifted their activities to neighboring states and "traveled around Guadalajara with platoons of guards armed with automatic weapons and with suitcases full of cash [with which] they bought whatever caught their fancy. Slow to bend to civilized ways, they lived like clannish hill people, marrying cousins, entertaining one another with raucous and violent parties, settling scores with impulsive savagery."

The Sinaloans eventually gained entrée into the cocaine business through Cuban-born Alberto Sicilia Falcón, who had become the überdon of cocaine. A flamboyant bisexual who made a big splash in the capital's social circles, Sicilia Falcón befriended Juan Ramón Matta Ballesteros, a shrewd Honduran chemist, who introduced the Cuban to Medellín boss Pablo Escobar. When the Federal Judicial Police (PJF), forerunner of the Federal Agency of Investigation (AFI), arrested Falcón in mid-1975, Matta Ballesteros knitted ties between the Colombians and the Sinaloan Félix Gallardo, who succeeded Sicilia as Mexico's top cocaine exporter.

Even as he maintained a home in Guadalajara, Félix Gallardo headed the mighty and expanding Sinaloa cartel, which observers call the "Blood Alliance" because of its leaders' family ties. These ties ensured a more cohesive organization than its Gulf counterpart—at least until the cataclysmic schism with the Beltrán Leyva brothers in 2007.

On the morning of April 8, 1989, Félix Gallardo awoke to confront a 12-man police task force. He offered them $5 or $6 million in exchange for his freedom but President Carlos Salinas (1988–94), who sought to ingratiate himself with Washington, gave strict orders to Federal Police Commander Guillermo González Calderoni to arrest the outlaw. An erstwhile compadre of Félix Gallardo, Calderoni complied and was killed for this "betrayal" in 2003 in Texas, where he had relocated. Although convicted of drug trafficking, bribery and illegal possession of weapons, the crafty Sinaloan still managed his lucrative empire from behind bars via a mobile phone, lawyers, visitors and prison guards until his transfer to a new maximum security facility in the 1990s.

Although incarcerated, Félix Gallardo distributed plazas and maintained order among his associates and underlings. Luis Héctor Palma Salazar and Guzmán Loera, along with the Beltrán Leyva brothers, took the reins of the Sinaloa operation. Félix Gallardo's nephews, the Arellano Félix brothers, eventually assumed control of the Tijuana cartel; Rafael Caro Quintero became *número uno* in Sonora; and Amado Carrillo Fuentes, nephew of Don Neto, held sway in Ciudad Juárez.

Thus Guzmán Loera rose to the top as one of the country's most prosperous underworld figures. In the late 1980s, the U.S. government successfully disrupted Colombian supply routes through south Florida and the Caribbean, forcing the Medellín and Cali cartels to find another avenue to the United States. They increasingly depended on Guzmán Loera and other Mexican gangsters to convey the narcotics to American consumers and thus, as Samuel Logan wrote in *The Power and Interest News Report*, the U.S.-Mexican border became the "soft underbelly" of drug commerce.

The Sinaloa cartel has traditionally controlled Acapulco's narcotics trade. Drug honchos owned posh waterfront homes, dined at luxurious bistros, vacationed in the area with their wives and children and avoided drawing attention to themselves. However, open warfare erupted in 2005 when the rival Gulf cartel sought retaliation for the Sinaloans' incursions into Nuevo Laredo and other venues along the Texas border that the Gulf brigands had claimed for themselves. The Gulf cartel dispatched its paramilitary force, Los Zetas, to gain revenge against its malevolent competitors.

Guzmán Loera took advantage of alternative drug routes through Central America that the Colombians had developed in the late 1980s and early 1990s to avoid radar detection. He also shifted from "muling" Colombian cocaine to taking ownership of it. He even dug sophisticated, carefully engineered tunnels to shuttle cocaine under the border. One of his accomplishments was excavating a 1,500-foot, concrete-reinforced, air-conditioned tunnel between Tijuana and Otay Mesa near San Diego. Guzmán Loera directed operations similar to those of a multinational corporation, but with a deadly difference. A federal drug agent who has tracked Guzmán Loera noted that "when Donald Trump calls you into the boardroom, you might lose your job. But when Chapo Guzmán calls you in, you might lose your life." In other words, "his business is crime."

In mid-2003, authorities arrested Guzmán Loera in Guatemala and sent him to prison for 20 years on charges of cocaine smuggling and bribery. He was linked to, but never charged with, the murder of Cardinal Juan Jesús Posadas Ocampo at the Guadalajara airport on May 24, 1993. The official version of the episode holds that gunmen from the Tijuana cartel mistook the prelate, garbed in civilian clothing and ensconced in a shiny black limousine, for Guzmán Loera, whom the Arellano Félix brothers had vowed to kill. Others regarded the murder as a warning to authorities that they should respect the "traditional understanding" between law-enforcement agencies and gangsters.

Public outrage forced federal authorities to pursue the drug barons, landing Guzmán Loera behind bars. Nevertheless, he continued to conduct transactions from a luxurious cell, where he imbibed fine wines, entertained prostitutes and chitchatted with Dan Rather and other media mavens. He kept in continual contact with his top lieutenant, Arturo Beltrán Leyva, and the other Beltrán Leyva brothers (Arturo "El Barbas," Alfredo "El Mochomo," Mario Alberto "El General" and Carlos). In January 2001, a few days before his scheduled extradition to the United States, Guzmán Loera broke out of the Puente Grande maximum security prison in Jalisco state, where he was serving a 20-year sentence for criminal association and bribery. The Beltrán Leyva brothers, along with Zambada, Esparragoza and dozens of other individuals, helped orchestrate this feat of derring-do, which made inventive use of a prison laundry cart after the inmate's electronically controlled cell door had flown open and video cameras ceased functioning.

Although it is unclear whether he or Arturo Beltrán Leyva was top dog, Guzmán Loera returned to his organization, possibly living on his ranch near La Tuna, a five-hour drive from Badiraguato. Guzmán Loera then ordered the killing of Rodolfo "Rodolfillo" Carrillo Fuentes, Amado's brother, who had been invading Guzmán Loera's trafficking routes and conniving with the Gulf cartel. The murder of Rodolfillo and his wife in Culiacán forced a meeting between Cárdenas Guillén and Guzmán Loera, who was advised that one of his brothers would die. Like any good soap opera, the plot thickened when a thug, allegedly acting on orders from Gulf cartel honcho Cárdenas Guillén, murdered Guzmán Loera's younger brother, Arturo, inside La Palma prison in late 2004.

By 2006, the Beltrán Leyva family had eliminated all competition across the 330 miles of Arizona border—supposedly by working with state government officials. A year later, the corridor from Sinaloa to Sonora to Arizona had become a bloody zone where at least 25 police, 40 killers and numerous border-crossing immigrants had perished.

In 2007 the Beltrán Leyvas became furious with El Chapo when he stridently opposed their establishing a separate cartel. Guzmán

Loera also learned that the would-be secessionists had agreed secretly with Heriberto Lazcano Lazcano, leader of Los Zetas, to take over and divide up El Chapo's territories. To show that he could play hardball, El Chapo framed a relative of the Beltrán Leyva brothers, Sandra Ávila Beltrán—"the Queen of the Pacific" and a key drug figure in her own right—whom authorities arrested on September 28, 2007.

The Beltrán Leyvas suffered a more severe blow on January 20, 2008, with the arrest of another brother, Alfredo "El Mochomo," who purportedly oversaw large-scale smuggling and money-laundering projects. *El Universal* reported that Arturo Beltrán Leyva held El Chapo personally responsible for his brother's capture, declared open warfare on Guzmán Loera and even began working with elements of the Gulf cartel on the theory that "the enemy of my enemy is my friend." The most notable casualty in this internecine conflict may have been El Chapo's son Edgar Guzmán, whom Beltrán Leyva's mobsters are believed to have executed in May 2008. In October 2008, authorities arrested Jesús Reynaldo "El Rey" Zambada García, brother of Sinaloa honcho Ismael "El Mayo" Zambada García, who was in a life-and-death struggle with the Beltrán Leyva crime family for dominion over drug flows through the crime-suffused Mexico City airport.

Yet, the debilitated Sinaloa cartel continues to do business throughout Mexico, along the southwest border, in the western and midwestern regions of the United States, as well as in Central America. Its traditional route ran from Chiapas to Ciudad Juárez, passing through nine or more states. The syndicate also imports cocaine via Lázaro Cárdenas and other Pacific ports from the remnants of the Medellín and Cali cartels—the so-called *cartelitos* scattered throughout Colombia. Besides smuggling cocaine, the enterprise distributes heroin from Mexico and Southeast Asia along with Mexican marijuana.

Its access to abundant marijuana supplies has provided the Sinaloans with an advantage over their Gulf adversaries because, as a rule, the U.S. Justice Department does not prosecute carriers apprehended with fewer than 500 grams of marijuana.

Rather than decry El Chapo as a lawbreaker, his neighbors venerate him for his largesse and the thousands of jobs created by poppy cultivation. "They see him as a hero. They cover for him. When any stranger comes into the communities, they warn him," observed the Deputy Attorney General José Luis Santiago Vasconcelos. A resident told the *Los Angeles Times:* "When the cops pass El Chapo on the road, they call him boss." He has become a folk hero extolled in songs.

The Sinaloans' claimed aversion to bloodletting aside, hundreds of innocent people perished in 2008 when the drug-related death toll in their state through early October had reached 454—compared with 346 in 2007 and 350 in 2006.

SONORA CARTEL

Founders: In the 1970s: Rafael Ángel Caro Quintero (arrested April 5, 1985) and Miguel Caro Quintero (arrested December 2001). These arrests severely weakened the organization.

Key Figures: Miguel Caro Quintero's siblings (Genaro, Jorge, María del Carmen, Blanca Lili, Melinda and Maria). However, Francisco "Dos Mil" Hernández García, leader of a gang known as "Los Números" and a former ally of the Sinaloans, has switched his loyalty to the Gulf cartel and is trying to recoup a plaza in the state.

Structure of Operations: The Sonora cartel, allied with the Sinaloans particularly through Caro Quintero's relationship with Félix Gallardo and Ernesto Fonseca, operates mainly in its own state and nearby border areas, utilizing small planes to fly marijuana, cocaine and methamphetamines to the United States. Caro Quintero, a native of Badriguato, Sinaloa, cultivated enormous marijuana plantations, complemented by huge drying sheds, in Sonora and neighboring Chihuahua. He paid off police commanders in both states so they would steer clear of his sophisticated industry. In November 1984 the federal police raided Caro Quintero's property at El Búfalo, Chihuahua, and destroyed between 5,000 and 10,000 tons of high-quality seedless marijuana, with a street value estimated at $2.5 billion. They were alerted to the site by DEA agent Enrique "Kiki" Camarena, who was subsequently tortured and murdered. (See Camarena case, p. 26.)

After the imprisonment of his brother Rafael, Miguel Ángel Caro Quintero took control of operations with his other two brothers and three sisters. They continue to specialize in marijuana cultivation on ranches in the north, still relying on small aircraft to shuttle the drug into Arizona. On December 20, 2001, authorities apprehended Miguel Ángel Caro Quintero with the goal of extraditing him to the United States.

A major drug-related event in Sonora occurred after midnight on May 16, 2007, when 15 trucks carrying men armed with AR-15 assault rifles rumbled into Cananea, a copper-mining town 20 miles south of the Mexico-Arizona border. The menacing convoy snaked through the sleepy Sonoran municipality for an hour before its gunmen killed five policemen and two civilians. The attackers then fled into the Sierra Madre mountains where they were tracked down by the PFP and local police. The incident concluded with the death of 23 individuals and left several wounded.

Public Safety Secretary García Luna attributed the mayhem to a turf battle between the Gulf cartel and its Sinaloa rival, with whom the Caro Quintero clan are traditional allies. Francisco "Dos Mil" Hernández García, who had aligned himself with the Gulf organization, may have been trying to gain a presence for his new masters. The episode ignited a shake-up of federal police in the state and ushered in months of relative tranquility in most of the state—except for the noisy takeoffs of drug-carrying Cessnas headed north and a spate of killings in Nogales, including state police commander Juan Manuel Pavón Félix. Genaro Caro Quintero, the cartel's presumed leader, has disappeared from sight.

MILENIO CARTEL

Founders: Armando "Juanito" Valencia Cornelio was the top dog until his arrest in mid-2003. Meanwhile, "Joint Operation Michoacán" (December 2006) succeeded in capturing four of his lieutenants.

Key Figures: Luis and Juan Valencia Cornelio operate a crippled organization. Destabilization in Michoacán has further weakened their power base, as *La Familia* or the Family, a multifaceted crime organization—originally in league with the Gulf cartel—has enlarged its diverse criminal activities.

Structure of Operations: The Milenio cartel began operations in the 1990s under the leadership of the Valencia Cornelio brothers—Armando and Juan—and their cousin Luis Valencia Valencia. They concentrated the operation in their home state of Michoacán, the entry point for a great deal of Colombian cocaine, as well as in Jalisco, Colima and Nayarit, while cooperating with the Sinaloans. Early in the decade, the DEA claimed that it supplied one third of all cocaine to the United States, with distribution focused on California, Texas, Chicago and New York. By mid-2003, Mexican authorities captured Armando "Juanito" Valencia Cornelio, the organization's ring master. His arrest bestowed leadership upon his brother Juan and cousin Luis, who is closer to the Beltrán Leyva brothers than to Guzmán Loera.

JALISCO CARTEL

Key Figure: Ignacio "Nacho" Coronel Villarreal.

Structure of Operations: Villarreal, who heads the Jalisco cartel, collaborates with Gúzman Loera's faction of the Sinaloa cartel. In December 2006, the federal government severely weakened this syndicate when it captured a half-dozen of Coronel's allies in Guadalajara. In information related to its $5 million reward for Coronel, the FBI noted that "the scope of its influence and operations [of Coronel's cartel] penetrate throughout the United States, Mexico and several other European, Central American and South American countries [and]...[it is] now considered one of the most powerful drug-trafficking organizations in Mexico...[working] directly with Colombian sources of supply by purchasing multi-ton quantities of cocaine." Known as the "Crystal King," Coronel Villarreal oversees the organization's methamphetamine operations from super-labs in Michoacán and Jalisco to supply a network that reaches from Nogales, Arizona, New Mexico and Texas to the U.S. eastern seaboard. His

Mexican structure stretches from Morelia, Michoacán, and along Mexico's Pacific coast through the states of Nayarit and Sinaloa and inland into Sonora.

COLIMA CARTEL

Founders/Key Figures: The Amézcua Contreras brothers (José de Jesús, Ignacio and Adán).

Structure of Operations: The Colima cartel, based in Guadalajara, was the chief supplier of methamphetamines to the United States. The brothers Jesús, Ignacio and Adán Amézcua Contreras earned fame as the "Kings of Meth." They began their criminal acts smuggling illegal aliens, turning their focus to methamphetamines and their precursor chemicals during the late 1980s and early 1990s while other Mexican cartels homed in on cocaine. Through a more organized and grander structure, the Colima cartel took over the previous motorcycle gangs and independent traffickers who had once dominated this trade. They manufactured meth in laboratories in Mexico and the United States from the precursor chemical ephedrine, which the cartel illegally imported from Germany, India, Thailand and Pakistan through the ports of Veracruz and Manzanillo. The capture and imprisonment of the Amézcua Contreras brothers in the late 1990s devastated the organization even though their sisters are trying to conduct business as usual.

Their wives are said to have needed to borrow bus fare to visit their spouses in prison. In contrast, the families of affluent drug dons incarcerated in La Palma prison in Mexico State have purchased luxurious homes in posh neighborhoods of nearby Mextepec, which has lofted real estate prices in the area.

GULF CARTEL

Founders: Juan Nepomuceno Guerra (died 2001); Juan García Abrego (close to Raúl Salinas—jailed and sent to the United States by Zedillo in January 1996); Salvador "El Chava" Gómez (killed in 1999, a victim of his friend Osiel Cárdenas Guillén, who wanted El Chava's territories); and Cárdenas Guillén (extradited to United States in January 2007) who earned the nickname "El Mata Amigos" or "Friend Killer" because of the allies he disposed of in order to enlarge his fiefdom.

Key Leaders: Power struggle among Eduardo "El Coss" Costilla Sánchez; Zeta leader Heriberto "The Executioner" Lazcano Lazcano; and Antonio Ezequiel "Tony Tormenta" Cárdenas Guillén.

Structure of Operations: The Gulf cartel is the main competitor of the Sinaloans. Juan Nepomuceno Guerra, who bootlegged whiskey to the United States during Prohibition, founded this organization in the early 1980s. Initially, the criminals focused on contraband, but Nepomuceno's nephew, Juan García Ábrego, expanded the enterprise to include cocaine. As with the Sinaloa cartel, the Colombians' need to ship cocaine through Mexico greatly enhanced the Gulf cartel's power and wealth in the mid-1980s. García Ábrego enjoyed success in part because of his collaboration with police commander González Calderoni. García Ábrego also worked with Quintana Roo Governor Mario Villanueva Madrid to facilitate the flow of drugs from the Yucatán peninsula through Campeche, Tabasco, Veracruz, Tamaulipas and ultimately to Nuevo León. The cartel operates primarily throughout Tamaulipas, Nuevo Laredo, Nuevo León and the Gulf coast to Quintana Roo, Michoacán and Guerrero.

In the aftermath of Cardinal Posada Ocampo's murder, Salinas cracked down on the Sinaloa and Arellano Félix organizations, but turned a blind eye to the delinquency of García Ábrego, who hobnobbed with the president's brother, Raúl. Soon after Ernesto Zedillo (1994–2000) succeeded Salinas, he ordered the arrest of García Ábrego. Following a discussion with his cabinet leaders, the president instructed authorities to hand over the lawbreaker to the FBI rather than imprison him in Mexico. This arrest sparked an intramural battle for gang leadership with Cárdenas Guillén winding up on top.

Although the police captured Cárdenas Guillén in Matamoros in March 2003, like other imprisoned cartel leaders, he continued to administer his organization from La Palma. The drug lords enjoyed comfortable prison accommodations, including TV sets, air conditioners, telephones, liquor and visits from wives and girlfriends. From their cells, they organized shameless stunts. In April 2006, Cárdenas treated 22,000 people to a "Children's Day" party at a baseball stadium in Reynosa, near McAllen, Texas. As the festivities wound down, two large vehicles lumbered in and distributed toys with notes saying they were from Cárdenas Guillén. An advertisement in *El Mañana* newspaper claimed that the big shot paid for the event, with a headline proclaiming that "Osiel makes thousands of children happy." He threw similar parties in Piedras Negras and Acuña, Coahuila, and as a result, Children's Day celebrations take place from Matamoros to Acuña every year.

The January 2007 extradition of Cárdenas Guillén to the United States set off a battle among three contenders to succeed him: Osiel's brother, Antonio Ezequiel "Tony Tormenta" Cárdenas Guillén, Eduardo "El Coss" Costilla Sánchez and Heriberto "The Executioner" Lazcano Lazcano, the top leader of Los Zetas. This last force has grown to include military and police personnel and appears to possess the strongest criminal organization in Tamaulipas, where corruption suffuses the government. They increasingly act on their own, trafficking drugs, charging "tolls" to other mafiosi who want to cross their territory, carrying out kidnappings, engaging in extortion, committing murders-for-hire and selling protection to businesses.

Many of Lazcano's earliest recruits received instruction in intelligence and high-powered weaponry while some even belonged to the U.S.-trained Airmobile Special Forces Group (GAFE). Los Zetas work with both brutal Central American gangs and Kaibiles, ruthless Guatemalan commandos, and operate in more than a dozen jurisdictions, including Mexico City and Michoacán. They have stocked safe houses with grenades, antitank weapons, assault rifles and other heavy armaments. Los Zetas have reportedly recruited young Hispanic gangs in Laredo, Texas—the so-called "zetitas"— to broaden their activities in the United States.

In Mexico, Los Zetas have formed the "Halcones" ("Falcons") composed of youngsters age twelve to seventeen. They serve as the eyes and ears of Los Zetas, hanging out on street corners to report any suspicious vehicle entering "their neighborhood." In border cities and in Culiacán, Los Zetas have brazenly unfurled eye-popping banners to attract active and retired soldiers to their cause, promising "a good salary, food, care for your family [and that] you will not be mistreated or suffer hunger." They have also begun to make common cause with the Beltrán Leyva brothers, the erstwhile comrades of El Chapo in Sinaloa, even as disputes intensify between El Coss and Tony Tormenta.

La Familia (the Family) in Michoacán originally joined forces with the Gulf cartel against its common enemies in Sinaloa. La Familia has split into four segments, only one of which now cooperates with Los Zetas. The surging hostility between this Michoacán syndicate and the Gulf lords may explain why the latter put up a $5 million reward for evidence leading to the capture of La Familia members who allegedly detonated the fragmentation grenades in Morelia, the capital of Michoacán and the starting point of Mexico's independence movement, on September 15, 2008. The newspaper *El Universal* reported that one or more elements of La Familia have penetrated the governments of 20 Michoacán municipalities, which represent one fifth of the state's territory. Their success arises from the suborning of local, state and federal officials. Dionisio "El Tío" Loya Plancarte reportedly manipulates the press, handles public relations and acts as a go-between on behalf of La Familia in its relations with politicians, the police and other criminal syndicates. Its leaders are religious fanatics Nazario Moreno González and Luis Méndez Vargas.

JUÁREZ CARTEL

Founders: DHS Commander Rafael Aguilar Guajardo guaranteed the takeover of Chihuahua by Félix Gallardo, who sent Amado Carrillo Fuentes to learn about the state from Pablo Acosta Villarreal, an operator in Ojinaga. After Acosta was killed in 1987, Guajardo assumed control until Carrillo Fuentes had him murdered in 1993. Since Amado's death in 1997, his brother Vicente Carrillo Fuentes has been the cartel's top capo.

Key Leader: Vicente Carrillo Fuentes.

Structure of Operations (Territorial Accords with Gulf Car-

tel): The Juárez cartel originated in the mid-1970s. Although still in business, this cartel has been greatly weakened amid rampant violence in its bailiwick. After Operation Condor (1977), five small organizations fought for supremacy over drug ventures in Chihuahua. Federal Commander Aguilar Guajardo eliminated these gangs to ensure the dominance of Félix Gallardo, whose right-hand man Amado Carrillo Fuentes supervised his cocaine shipments. After the 1989 arrest of Félix Gallardo, Carrillo Fuentes ascended to número uno in 1993, after having Aguilar Guajardo killed. At one point, he was exporting four times more cocaine to the United States than any other trafficker. He was called "the Lord of the Skies" for his deft use of a fleet of 727 aircraft to transport Colombian cocaine to municipal airports and dirt airstrips throughout Mexico.

Carrillo Fuentes also had links to Medellín and Cali kingpins. His organization specialized in trafficking cocaine, heroin and marijuana, with bases in Guadalajara, Hermosillo and Torreón, where drugs were stored and later shipped to the United States. In the mid-1990s, the cartel reportedly generated billions of dollars a year in illegal profits and had forwarded $20 million to $30 million dollars to Colombia for each major operation. It even began expanding into traditional Colombian strongholds on the U.S. east coast. The police launched a concerted manhunt for the multimillionaire, who jetted to Russia, Cuba and other countries in search of a safe haven.

A low-keyed diplomatic figure, Carrillo Fuentes concluded accords with rival cartels and even managed to ensnare General Jesús Gutiérrez Rebollo, whom President Ernesto Zedillo had appointed as the director of the National Institute to Combat Drugs (INCD), roughly the equivalent of the DEA, in December 1996. Praised by U.S. officials, the 42-year army veteran was called upon to clean up antidrug police agencies. Washington's drug czar, Gen. Barry McCaffrey, lauded Gutiérrez Rebollo as "a guy of absolute unquestioned integrity." Despite initial efforts at a cover-up, military authorities arrested the general on February 18, 1997. Deemed a model officer by many of his peers, he was convicted of working for the Juárez cartel and sentenced to 71 years in prison.

Gutiérrez Rebollo engraved an enduring mark on Mexico's criminal landscape. During his brief tenure at the INCD, he dispatched his loyalists to the institute's local offices, especially in the north. If they had been clean before arriving, these officials were soon corrupted. Another spawning ground for Los Zetas was the local branch of the Attorney General's Office, where, in 1995 under "pilot plan" Chihuahua, Zedillo and his Chief Prosecutor Jorge Madrazo Cuéllar substituted military men for members of the venal Federal Judicial Police.

Carrillo Fuentes died in mid-1997 while undergoing facial plastic surgery and stomach liposuction to change his appearance. The "Lord of the Skies" was honored at a large and costly funeral in his hometown of Guamuchilito, Sinaloa, where the people revered him as a kind of "Robin Hood." He was known for giving away money, cattle and presents, including expensive automobiles, to hundreds of people. Though condemned as a drug lord by federal agents, friends and family lauded Carrillo as "a noble soul, loving with his family," a simple man who "loved baseball and enchiladas stuffed with hot red chile."

Esparragoza, who temporarily replaced Carrillo Fuentes, reportedly tried to forge a pact with Sinaloan bosses Gúzman Loera and Zambada: the former would move into the Tamaulipas drug trade and the latter would wrest from the Tijuana cartel the smuggling routes into California. This arrangement did not bear fruit and after several kaleidoscopic changes, Carrillo Fuentes's brother Vicente took the reins of the debilitated organization. This vacuum attracted a no-holds-barred war between the Sinaloa and Gulf cartels that shows no sign of ending.

TIJUANA CARTEL/ ARELLANO FÉLIX ORGANIZATION (AFO)

Founders: After the arrest of Félix Gallardo, power devolved to (1) Javier Caro Payán, who (2) was displaced by Jesús "El Chuy" Labra, (3) whose capture placed control of the cartel in the hands of his nephews, the Arellano Félix brothers. Authorities apprehended the oldest brother Francisco Rafael Arellano

Félix (1993); imprisoned the group's CEO, Ismael "El Mayel" Higuera Guerro (2000); killed Ramón Arellano Félix (2002); arrested Benjamín Arellano Félix (2002); captured Javier Arellano Félix (2006); and apprehended Eduardo "The Doctor" Arellano Félix (2008).

Key Figures: The arrest of Eduardo leaves Enedina Arellano Félix as the clan's titular head. She is weak due to her inability to control the cartel loyalists of Benjamín, the only family member who could maintain discipline. Former underlings of Benjamín are staking out their own plazas: Jorge "El Cholo" Briseño López (Rosarito) and Eduardo "El Teo" García Simental (Tecate area). Eduardo Gustavo Rivera Martínez had held sway in Ensenada until his March 2008 arrest. Enedina's son Fernando "The Engineer" Sánchez Arellano is locked in a battle for control of the hugely fragmented organization with García Simental. After serving sentences in Mexico and the U.S., Washington extradited Francisco Rafael to Mexico in March 2008.

Structure of Operations: Launched after the 1989 arrest of Félix Gallardo, like several other cartels, the ability of the Tijuana/AFO cartel to ship cocaine through Mexico greatly increased its power and wealth in the mid-1990s. The killing and arrest of leaders, combined with its loss of access to cocaine, have prompted the AFO to diversify its criminal ventures. The main base of its operations is in Tijuana, Baja California, and it has branches in parts of Sinaloa, Sonora, Jalisco and Tamaulipas. Difficulty in obtaining Colombian cocaine, combined with the deaths and arrests of several brothers, have severely weakened the organization. They have turned to recruiting youngsters from well-to-do Tijuana families to practice torture, assassinations and dismemberment.

The middle-class couple, Francisco Arellano Sánchez and Alicia Isabel Félix Azueta, raised 10 (some sources indicate 11) children in Sinaloa, four of whom (Francisco Rafael, Benjamín, Ramón and Francisco Javier) dedicated themselves to smuggling clothing and electronic goods before entering the drug trade. Benjamín attracted the attention of Javier Caro Payán, a lieutenant of Félix Gallardo. After the arrest of Félix Gallardo, Caro Payán, who had been awarded the Tijuana plaza, was forced to flee the country only to be arrested in Canada. Jesús "El Chuy" Labra Áviles and his nephew, Benjamín Arellano Félix, filled the vacuum left by Caro Payán's absence. This coup against Payán, a cousin of Caro Quintero, gave rise to the lingering and intense enmity between the AFO and the Sinaloa and Sonora cartels.

Until his arrest on March 12, 2000, "El Chuy" headed the organization, which specialized in selling protection to business and political leaders. Benjamín functioned as chief strategist, while Ramón spearheaded violence against their foes. They also telegraphed clear messages to those who attempted to utilize the Mexicali/Tijuana corridor without paying the transit tax demanded by the Arellano-Felix syndicate. Extending its tentacles from Tijuana to the streets of San Diego, observers once considered the AFO the most violent of the Mexican crime families. This organization maintained well-armed and highly trained security contingents that Mexican officials describe as paramilitary in character, including international mercenaries serving as advisers, trainers and members.

In 2000, authorities captured Higuera Guerrero and "Chuy" Labra; in 2002, the police killed Ramón; police arrested Benjamín—the real power in the cartel—later in the same year; and four years later, the U.S. Coast Guard captured the flamboyant Francisco Javier. These setbacks left the two university-educated members of the family, Eduardo, who is now in custody, and his sister Enedina, an accountant, as nominal heads of a debilitated cartel. Benjamín's loyalists are staking out their own territories. The AFO now faces difficulties acquiring cocaine from Colombia through its established network, which had once extended from the Guatemalan-Chiapas border through the western states to Tijuana. Nonetheless, the DEA believes that the Arellano Felix brothers excavated massive and sophisticated tunnels under the California-Mexico border in January 2006.

Jesús Blancornelas, a prize-winning journalist with *Zeta*, the Tijuana weekly, has argued that those setbacks aside, the AFO remains a potent force thanks to its corporate structure. He claimed that Gustavo Rivera Martínez, a U.S. citizen, took charge of day-to-day affairs, and that the cartel's business-like orientation enabled it to contact any of its regional representatives within an hour. In March 2008, the authorities who arrested Rivera Martínez with three alleged colleagues in the state of Baja California Sur announced plans immediately to send the 46-year-old suspect to the United States.

The AFO has challenged the Mexican state more than any other cartel. Involved in the death of Cardinal Posadas Ocampo in 1993, it precipitated a wave of killings when Zedillo flew to Baja California in 2000 to reaffirm his fight against organized crime. The AFO also cultivated contacts with Colombia's FARC guerrillas, as well as criminal organizations in Peru, Venezuela and the United States. It is now a fragmented, disorganized and virtually leaderless syndicate, composed of mafiosi whose defensiveness has enhanced their viciousness.

Recent arrests and fewer opportunities to dispatch cocaine northward have prompted the AFO to diversify its skullduggery: it has embarked upon kidnappings, auto thefts, extortion, murders-for-hire, human smuggling and other heinous felonies. Purportedly, Enedina Arellano Félix's son, Fernando Sánchez Arellano, is battling Eduardo "El Teo" García Simental for control of the cartel. El Teo claims support from El Chapo Guzmán and El Mayo Zambada, while Los Zetas, the Beltrán Leyva brothers and Vicente Carrillo Fuentes are believed to have cast their lot with The Engineer and his family. As a result, Tijuana has become one of the most dangerous cities in the Americas.

The mayhem has hit Tijuana's tourism like a sledgehammer. Still, the funeral industry is booming. Reuters reported that morticians from other parts of the country are opening branches in this border city. Shootouts and beheadings have spurred demand for facial reconstructions, and some funeral parlors charge more than $1,000 to make bodies presentable for wakes. In light of the surge in decapitations, many undertakers have agreed to hold the body and wait for the head to be found before proceeding with the open-casket service.

APPENDIX 2
Calderón's Major Antidrug Operations

MICHOACÁN I (Meager results led quickly to Michoacán II) December 10, 2006.
Personnel: Initial deployment of 6,784 personnel: 4,260 soldiers, 1,054 marines, 1,420 federal police and 50 federal detectives.
Goal: To eradicate drug cultivation and to combat by land, sea and air the cartels including Los Valencias, Los Zetas and La Familia.
Results: Marijuana and poppy fields destroyed, weapons seized, boats and vehicles confiscated and 1,301 suspects arrested, including Alfonso "Ugly Poncho" Barajas, a low-level leader of a unit of Los Zetas.

TIJUANA January 1, 2007.
Personnel: 1, 242 federal police and soldiers.
Goal: To restore order in a city beset by murders and kidnappings by the AFO, which transports cocaine to the United States.
Results: 2,443 suspects arrested.

GUERRERO January 13, 2007.
Personnel: 7,600 federal police, army and marines.
Goal: To try to end the horrendous murders, especially in Acapulco.
Results: Arrested 494 suspects. Seized weapons, vehicles, communications equipment and police uniforms.

GOLDEN TRIANGLE/SIERRA MADRE (CHIHUAHUA, DURANGO AND SINALOA) February 13, 2007.
Personnel: 9,054 soldiers, 40 airplanes, 20 helicopters and 25 trained dogs.
Goal: To destroy marijuana crops and collect weapons and vehicles used by narco-traffickers.
Results: 442 surveillance flights facilitated the destruction of 3,151 hectares of marijuana and poppy, as well as two laboratories; 2,188 suspects arrested; weapons, aircraft and $34,000 seized.

NUEVO LEÓN-TAMAULIPAS February 17, 2007.
Personnel: 3,499 soldiers; three airplanes and six helicopters.
Goal: To capture members of the Gulf cartel and Los Zetas.
Results: 1,396 suspects arrested.

TABASCO March 17, 2007.
Personnel: 200 PFP and 20 members of the army.
Goal: To rein in drug activities believed to be spearheaded by local law-enforcement officials who belonged to the shadowy "La Hermandad" or "The Brotherhood."
Results: Three police chiefs and a state official were arrested.

DRAGON Early and mid-2007.
Personnel: DEA authorities in cooperation with the PGR.
Goal: DEA agents captured Chinese-Mexican chemical importer Zhenli Ye Gon in Maryland on July 23, 2007; previously, authorities had found in his luxurious D.F. homes $227 million in cash and travelers' checks. In addition, the PGR discovered a cache of expensive automobiles, high-powered rifles and equipment to make amphetamine pills.

MICHOACÁN II Spring-Summer 2007.
Personnel: 4,579 federal police and soldiers.
Goal: To curb murders and kidnappings as gangs compete for drug routes.

VERACRUZ May 11, 2007.
Personnel: 1,200 PFP and soldiers.
Goal: To affirm the rule of law in the aftermath of the murder of four bodyguards protecting the three sons of Mexico State Governor Enrique Peña Nieto.
Results: 225 suspects arrested

SONORA May 16, 2007.
Personnel: PFP and soldiers.
Goal: To suppress the raging turf battle between the Gulf and

Sinaloa cartels.
Results: 3,833 suspects arrested since December 1, 2006.

MICHOACÁN III October 20, 2007.
Personnel: 100 members of the military, the AFI and the PFP.
Goal: To quell narco-activities in the state, with a focus on the port of Lázaro Cárdenas through which cocaine and precursor drugs enter Mexico.

MANZANILLO (COLIMA) October 30, 2007.
Personnel: Navy, PFP, army, Customs and AFI.
Goal: To thwart illegal drug shipments.
Results: Found 23 tons and 562 kilograms of cocaine in a container vessel that had arrived from Colombia—the largest such seizure ever recorded.

TAMAULIPAS "NORTHEAST OPERATION" January 22, 2008.
Personnel: Hundreds of GAFE troops.
Goal: To relieve local police of duty; disarmed their officers in Nuevo Laredo, Matamoros and Reynosa as army troops searched for evidence that might link them to ever-more violent drug traffickers in the state.

TAMAULIPAS-NUEVO LEÓN February 28, 2008.
Personnel: 110 soldiers of the Special Forces 10th battalion.
Goal: To combat intra-cartel violence sparked by Gulf Cartel as several lieutenants sought to take charge after Osiel Cárdenas' extradition.

MANZANILLO (COLIMA) March 6, 2008.
Personnel: Navy, Customs and federal police.
Goal: To intercept illegal goods and cash.
Results: Seized nearly $12 million in U.S. bills, which originated in Toluca and were on a ship bound for Panama, a major transshipment point for Colombian traffickers.

SOUTHERN AREA "CLEAN-UP OPERATION" March 2008.
Personnel: Army and civilian authorities.
Goal: To prevent small aircraft from ferrying drugs to Mexico from Colombia, Venezuela and Panama.

JOINT JUÁREZ March 23, 2008.
Personnel: 485 soldiers from D.F., including 200 members of the Corps of Special Forces who belonged to the Parachute Brigade. At least three Guatemalan commandos known as Kaibiles assisted in the strike. Hercules C-130, Boeing 727 and Barreta .50 mm machine gun employed.
Goal: 42 individuals, 37 weapons and 51 vehicles seized, along with quantities of cocaine, marijuana, heroin and meth. 1,044 suspects arrested since February 13, 2007.

CHIHUAHUA March 27, 2008 (reinforcements in April).
Personnel: 400 federal police; military provided 2,526 troops, 180 tactical vehicles, 3 aircraft; 46 mobile control posts sent to violence-beset Ciudad Juárez.
Goal: To quell mounting and unprecedented bloodshed sparked by turf battle between Sinaloa and Juárez cartels.
Results: Captured several big shots belonging to the Juárez cartel, as well as armored vehicles and high-powered weapons.

TIJUANA, CIUDAD JUÁREZ AND CULIACÁN May 10, 2008.
Personnel: Armed forces and federal, state and local police.
Goal: Combat the proliferation of drug-realted violence—exacerbated by inter-cartel strife—in these three cities.

CULIACÁN-NAVOLATO May 13, 2008.
Personnel: In three stages, more than 3,000 members of the armed forces and federal police; encountered severe resistance from drug traffickers believed to be Beltran Leyva loyalists, as well as from local police; General Rodolfo Cruz López, who commanded the action, complained that the criminals had more lethal weapons than his troops.

Goal: To pursue capos of Sinaloa cartel.
Results: Captured 6 tons and 280 kilos of marijuana, 425 kilos of cocaine, troves of weapons and vehicles and $5.3 million in cash.

MEXICO CITY July 23, 2008.
Personnel: Federal police, the PGR and customs.
Goal: To minimize smuggling through the Benito Juárez International Airport.
Results: Seizure of $2 million from a commercial flight bound for Cali, Colombia.

MICHOACÁN IV July 28, 2008.
Personnel: Federal police and soldiers from the 21st Military Zone.
Goal: To stem the contagion of kidnappings that had reached 30 by late July 2008, compared with 33 during all of 2007.
Results: The army confiscated high-powered weapons, ammunition and fragmentation grenades, while dismantling a house that served as an operations' center for extortionists.

TABASCO September 5, 2008.
Personnel: The army's 17th Infantry Battalion and federal police took control of the municipality of Cárdenas.
Goal: To reduce the firepower of criminal organizations linked to police in 11 of the state's 17 municipalities.
Results: Captured scores of rifles and pistols, as well as military equipment and 13 vehicles. Soldiers confined state police to their headquarters in order to inspect their weapons; authorities took the director of the state police to Mexico City for questioning.

MICHOACÁN V September 15-16, 2008.
Personnel: Soldiers from the 21st Military Zone, Federal, state and local police.
Goal: To restore order and apprehend the culprits who threw two fragmentation grenades into a large crowd in Morelia amid the September 15 Independence Day celebration.

PROJECT RECKONING September 16, 2008.
Personnel: Italian authorities; U.S. agencies, including the Justice Department, DEA, FBI, Internal Revenue Service, Marshals Service. (During his visit to Italy in 2007, President Calderón discussed with local law-enforcement officials cooperation on drug issues.)
Goal: To crack an international drug and money-laundering scheme.
Results: Seized $60 million and 40 tons of narcotics, and 175 suspects, including second-tier members of the Gulf cartel.

MAPACHE October 8, 2008.
Personnel: PGR (SIEDO).
Goal: To shut down a complex network, involving the shipment of drugs from Mexico to Atlanta, Philadelphia and Indiana.
Results: Captured Wenceslao "El Wencho" Álvarez Álvarez, an operator for both the Gulf cartel and La Familia.

CLEANING (LIMPIEZA) Late Summer/Fall 2008.
Personnel: Attorney General's Office.
Goal: Apprehension of former SIEDO chief Noë Ramírez Mandujano and other high-level law-enforcement agents for taking huge bribes to leak information to cartels.

CHIHUAHUA November 2008.
Personnel: 1,200 troops of army's airborne and motorized brigades.
Goal: Diminish the wave of violence pounding the state and especially Ciudad Juárez.

APPENDIX 3
Mexico's Security Cabinet

■ **SPECIAL ADVISER TO PRESIDENT CALDERÓN ON SE-CURITY MATTERS**

Jorge Enrique Tello Peón, born May 22, 1956, Yucatán.

Education and Background: Degrees in hydraulic engineering (UNAM) and civil engineering (UAM); Masters in Public Administration (Centro de Investigación Y Docencia Económica). During 20 years of government service, participated in the creation of CISEN, CENDRO, INCD and the PFP; since 2001, worked as vice president of international intelligence for planning and finance in multinational giant, Cementos Mexicanos, where he was responsible for a worldwide system of Strategic Information

■ **ATTORNEY GENERAL (PGR)**

Eduardo Medina Mora Icaza, born January 30, 1957, Federal District.

Education and Background: Law degree (UNAM).

Various private-sector and government posts, including director general of CISEN (2000-2005) and Secretary of Public Security (2005-2006).

■ **DEPUTY ATTORNEY GENERAL FOR JUDICIAL AND INTERNATIONAL AFFAIRS**

Juan Miguel Alcántara Soria, born March 18, 1955, Irapuato, Guanajuato State.

Education and Background: Law degree (Escuela Libre de Derecho); graduate studies (University of Complutense, Instituto Universitario Ortega y Gasset).

Private Practice; Attorney General for Guanajuato (1991-96); federal deputy (1997-2000; 1988-91); Guanajuato state legislator (1994-97); law professor; and various positions in the PAN, which he joined in 1970.

- **DEPUTY ATTORNEY GENERAL FOR THE SPECIAL-IZED INVESTIGATION OF ORGANIZED CRIME (SIEDO)**
Marisela Morales Ibáñez, born March 1, 1970, Federal District.
Education and Background: Law degree (UNAM); advanced study (National Institute of Criminal Studies).

Various positions in the PGR: Director of Investigations of Crimes Committed (1996-97); Chief of Specialized Fiscal Unit (1997-2001); General Coordinator of Investigations, including responsibility for gathering evidence related to the murder of Cardinal Posadas Ocampo, and close collaborator of Attorney General Rafael Macedo de la Concha with whom she worked on the *desafuero* (loss of right to seek public office) of Federal District mayor Andrés Manuel López Obrador 2001-2005; Coordinator of Ministerios Públicos or federal investigators (2005-2006); and enjoys good relations with the armed forces.

- **DEPUTY ATTORNEY GENERAL FOR REGIONAL CON-TROL AND PENAL PROCEDURES**
Víctor Emilio Corzo Cabañas, born October 22, 1949.
Education and Background: Law Degree (UNAM).

Adjunct director general, CISEN: Ministry of Tourism (technical secretary in the Office of the Secretary; PGR, director general of legal and international affairs.

- **DEPUTY ATTORNEY GENERAL FOR INVESTIGATION OF FEDERAL CRIMES**
Felipe de Jesús Muñoz Vázquez, born July 12, 1959, Aguascalientes, Aguas.
Education and Background: Law Degree (UNAM); postgraduate studies in police science.

Career in PGR, including chief of unit specialized in crimes against the rights of authors and industrial property; subdelegate in Quintana Roo, head of unit specialized in investigating fiscal and financial crimes; and director general of investigations (Ministerio Público "A").

- **CHIEF OF PLANNING, DEVELOPMENT, AND INSTITU-TIONAL INNOVATION (PGR)**
Ardelio Vargas Fosado, born January 14, 1955, Xicotepec de Juárez, Puebla.
Education and Background: Law degree (UNAM—Enep/Acatlán).
PFP (2005-07); CISEN (1994–2005); mayor of Xicotepec de Juárez (1987–90); and close ties to Medina Mora.

- **SECRETARY OF PUBLIC SECURITY (SSP)**
Genaro García Luna, born July 10, 1968, Federal District.
Education and Background: Degree in mechanical engineering. (U. Autónoma Metropolitana)
Director of AFI (2005–2006); general coordinator of intelligence for prevention in PFP (1998–2000); CISEN (1989–98). In December 2008, Javier del Real Magallanes, age 63, was named subsecretary for strategy and police intelligence, bringing a senior general into a top SSP post.

- **SECRETARY OF NATIONAL DEFENSE (SEDENA)**
Gen. Guillermo Galván Galván, born January 19, 1943, Federal District.
Education and Background: Heroíco Colegio Militar.
Various army commands.

- **SECRETARY OF THE NAVY (SEMAR)**
Adm. Mariano Francisco Saynez Mendoza, born September 20, 1942, Veracruz, Veracruz.
Education and Background: Heroíca Escuela Naval Militar.
Various naval commands.

- **SECRETARY OF GOVERNMENT (SEGOB)**
Fernando Francisco Gómez Mont Urueta, born January 11, 1963, Federal District.
Education and Background: Law degree (Escuela Libre de

Derecho); son of PAN founding ideologue; Federal deputy (1991-94); adviser to President Zedillo on judicial issues; worked with Attorney General Antonio Lozano Gracias on various matters including the deaths of Luis Donaldo Colosio and José Francisco Ruiz Massieu; member of prestigious Zínser Esponda and Gómez Mont law firm that has defended such controversial clients as Raúl Salinas; and close to pragmatic PAN notables like former senator and super-lawyer Diego "El Jefe" Fernández de Cevallos.

■ **DIRECTOR OF CENTER FOR RESEARCH ON NATIONAL SECURITY (CISEN)**
Guillermo Valdés Castellanos, born May 24, 1955, Guadalajara, Jalisco.
Education and Background: Degree in social sciences (ITAM).
Adviser to his friend Calderón in presidential campaign; director of polling and consulting company, GEA-ISA; held positions in the ministries of Social Development, Planning and Budget and Public Education.

■ **EXECUTIVE SECRETARY OF MEXICO'S NATIONAL PUBLIC SECURITY SYSTEM (SNSP)**, which is under the formal jurisdiction of the National Public Safety Council (CNSP.) (Composed of the president and presided over by the secretary of public security, the CNSP includes the attorney general, the 32 governors, and the secretaries of government, national defense, and navy. As part of the Crime Prevention Strategy, the secretaries of education, health, social development and communications and transport may meet with the CNSP).
Monte Alejandro Rubido García, born January 27, 1954, Federal District.
Education and Background: Law degree (UNAM); M.A. in political science (U. of Paris).
Known as an "old sea wolf" because of his involvement in shadowy activities; worked in Gobernación in a subordinate post under

Secretary Fernando Gutiérrez Barrios; participated in the formation of CISEN (1989) and served in several posts in the intelligence agency, including director of strategic studies, adjunct secretary general and secretary general; extremely close to ex-Gobernación Secretary Emilio Chuayffet Chemor (1995–98) under whom he created the Office of Analysis and Investigation; in mid-2001 his name arose when the PGR dismantled an espionage ring in México State then governed by Arturo Montiel. In 2003, allies of Elba Esther Gordillo, head of the tremendously rich and powerful SNTE teachers' union accused CISEN and its secretary general, Rubido García, of taping 45 of her phone conversations, which were later published as Elba de Troya or Lady Macbeth Gordillo; subsecretary of prevention, coordination, and human rights at SPP (February 2007–September 2008); expert in the Chiapas-based Zapatista Nacional Liberation Army (EZLN) that declared war against the Mexican government on January 1, 1994.

■ **TECHNICAL SECRETARY OF NATIONAL SECURITY COUNCIL/CSN** (Composed of the president, the attorney general, CISEN, and the secretaries of government, public security, national defense, navy, foreign relations, finance, public function and communication and transport.)

Sigrid Arzt Colunga, born June 15, 1965, Federal District.

Education and Background: M.A. in international relations and peace studies (Notre Dame); completing Ph.D. thesis in comparative politics and international relations (U. of Miami).

Founder and current director of Democracia, Derechos Humanos y Seguridad Indiana; visiting professor at Georgetown U. under the auspices of the Woodrow Wilson Center; taught in the Centro de Estudios del Ejército y Fuerza Aerea and other Mexican universities; consultant on security matters; member of the PGR technical secretariat.